W9-AFI-564

THE DYNAMICS OF TEAM TEACHING

NICHOLAS C. POLOS, Ph.D.

Claremont, California

WM. C. BROWN COMPANY PUBLISHERS
135 SOUTH LOCUST STREET • DUBUQUE, IOWA 52003

Copyright © 1965
by
Wm. C. Brown Company Publishers

Library of Congress Catalog Number: 65-17724

Manufactured by WM. C. BROWN CO. INC., Dubuque, Iowa
Printed in U. S. A.

PREFACE

A great deal of skepticism surrounds team teaching, and this is due to the fact that it is very difficult to make completely accurate judgements about any enterprise which is in its fundamental stages. Team teaching is not *fait accompli* but is instead in the process of becoming. This analysis of team teaching therefore is not the final word on this important development in American education.

Much of the literature on team teaching projects is in the form of the "testimonial," and as such is often subjective, personal, and not always significant as field research. This analysis is a fresh, brief, concise picture of those team teaching projects which the author judges to be especially significant. It is not a defense for team teaching but instead attempts to come to grips with the many problems which team teaching raises. This is a pioneer approach in a pioneer field, and it is natural that many questions will be left unanswered and that there may be errors in both judgement and analysis. We must recognize, however, that we are in a "twilight" zone of American education here and that perhaps time will present us with a more accurate and sharpened image of team teaching.

This is an attempt to portray team teaching in its true light, as seen by educators actively engaged in the projects. In the sifting-out process, performed in order to present the reader with a "working" knowledge of the team teaching projects, every effort has been made to avoid the stilted phrases of any Procrustean educational philosophy which have too often in the past made discussions of educational improvement sterile.

Perhaps the author has magnified the importance of team teaching in trying to fit it into the general pattern of the needs of American education. Many think, however, that it is a novel approach, a possible vehicle for change, and as such is worth examining critically. This is only one part of a critical analysis, which also tries to take away the lollipops of self-delusion while avoiding the clucking of empty clichés. This study of team teaching, based on fact rather than unsupported opinions, raises many questions which the reader may find thought-provoking as well as pertinent to team teaching.

March, 1965   Nicholas C. Polos

CONTENTS

TO ETHEL WHO BELIEVES IN
EDUCATION FOR THE FUTURE

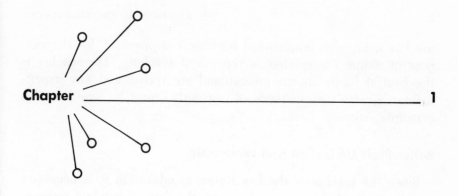

Chapter ———————————————————————————— 1

THE EXPLOSION IN EXPERIMENTATION

In 1775, Francis Hopkinson published "An Improved Plan of Education" in the Pennsylvania *Magazine*. In this plan he proposed "to lighten the labor of both pupils and teachers by teaching all subjects through games." In describing his plan Hopkinson wrote: "In like manner, may the young scholar be instructed in 'arithmetic,' by the healthful play of hop-scot . . . 'history and chronology' by a pack of cards."[1]

We cannot afford such a luxury today. America's power and new responsibilities in the family of nations is revolutionizing American education. The focus is on change, and this is understandable. "We are," writes Walter Lippmann, "entering upon a era which will test to the utmost the capacity of our democracy to cope with the gravest problems of modern times." In this era of experimentation, educational leaders are responding to the challenge by investigating new ways to prepare teachers, new methods of instruction, and the proper methods of incorporating new technological techniques into our schools.

The Teacher the Key Figure in Education

One thing must be clear to all of us in American education. If we introduce machine operations, i.e., educational television, teaching machines, directional image projectors, and various types of audio-

---

[1] Edgar W. Knight, "An Improved Plan of Education, 1775," *School and Society*, LXIX, No. 1799 (June 11, 1949), 409-11.

machines, into our educational horizon it is primarily for the purpose of aiding the teacher in the job of teaching. The teacher is
the central figure in our educational enterprise, and any experimentation with new methods of instruction must be based on this
principle.

Better Staff Utilization and Leadership

Since the teacher is the key figure in education it is necessary
to use our teaching personnel wisely; the "teaching talent reserve"
is low today. Francis Keppel has pointed out that "almost 10 percent of U. S. teachers leave the profession each year, that at any
given time half the American children are being taught by relatively inexperienced teachers. . .The temper of the times seems to
be right for experimentation and innovation in education."

There is another important reason for conserving the energies
of our teachers. "The function of a teacher," says Alexander Meikle-
john, "is to stand before his pupils and before the community at
large as the intellectual leader of his time. If he is not able to. . .
take this leadership he is not worthy of his calling." Obviously, the
teacher can hardly be an intellectual leader collecting milk money,
filling out endless administrative reports, grading innumerable
daily papers, and teaching in a "not so splendid isolation."

The Challenge of New Problems

Many schools throughout the nation are confronted with a triad
of problems: increasing enrollments, lack of adequate classroom
space, and the shortage of qualified teachers. When the cold war
moved into outer space, the American people became more disturbed than ever about these problems. They have attempted to respond creatively to these changing needs and circumstances and
to seek a partial cure by formulating plans for teacher's aides as
exemplified by the Bay City, Michigan, and Fairfield, Connecticut,
experiments.

Teacher Aide Plan

Several years ago in order to free the teacher and thus "improve
the quality of education," New York City, Utah, Colorado, Iowa,

and Minnesota put into operation some form of the plan for teachers' aides. This use of aides, about which more will be said later, was a distinct departure from the past, particularly from the monitorial system that flourished in the United States a century or so ago, in which aides were used to educate large numbers of children inexpensively — and inadequately.

Team Teaching Is Not a Panacea

One outgrowth of the teacher-aide plans is team teaching. "Team teaching" has become a magic phrase today; it is the genie of Aladdin's educational magic lamp, and, for some, the automatic escalator to an educational Utopia! Unfortunately, there are no easy answers to the complex problems associated with American education and its conduct, and it always seems easier to advocate the acceptance of a new idea rather than to study it, evaluate it, and improve it. Here an attempt will be made to destroy the stereotypes that are developing around the concepts of team teaching.

Team Teaching Antecedents

Carl H. Peterson calls team teaching an *avant-garde* program, and argues that it is here to stay.[2] Only time can determine the latter, but as to the former phrase, unless Mr. Peterson is thinking of a modified form of team teaching, the concept itself is not a new one. The historical stream of continuity denies the "fadistic" claim of some American educators.

Old Wine in a New Bottle

The term itself may be new, appearing in educational literature around 1957, but the Platoon School, the Winnetka Plan, and the Pueblo Plan all contained some of the characteristics of the modern team teaching concept. Perhaps this is why historians are fond of the line in Ecclesiastes which reads: ". . .and that which is done is that which shall be done: and there is no new thing under the sun."

Historically, for example, in the 1930's we find the Cooperative Group Plan, formulated by J. F. Hosic, a most recent prototype

---

[2]See Carl H. Peterson, "Is Team Teaching For Your Schools?"*American School Board Journal*, CXLV (October, 1962), 11-13.

of the team teaching plan. In regard to this plan, S. E. Dean wrote: ". . .small groups of teachers together organized the work for a group of children within a range of not more than three grades, and each group had its own chairman who also served in a supervisory capacity."[3] This was a much better team teaching situation than much of the "marginal team teaching" done today!

The Experimentation Explosion

Team teaching is a stimulating concept, and many schools in the nation have become "team teaching" conscious, so much so that it would be almost impossible to describe the many variations of team teaching that are being proposed and used by schools and educators today.[4] Since 1957 when the team teaching explosion began there has been an extensive series of experiments with the plan. Some of these have been supported by grants to the Commission on the Experimental Study of the Utilization of the Staff in the Secondary School, which was appointed by the National Association of Secondary School Principals and supported by the Fund for the Advancement of Education. The common features and results of these experiments are well reported in the National Association of Secondary School Principals *Bulletin*. This is a gold mine of team teaching information. Many of the schools are linked with universities such as Harvard, Chicago, Stanford, Wisconsin, Claremont Graduate School, and the University of Maine.

SUPRAD Projects

The school systems, for example, of Concord, Lexington, and Newton, Massachusetts, have joined Harvard University in the School and University Program for Research and Development. This is known as SUPRAD, and is responsible for some of the original projects in team teaching (The Franklin School Experiment). Dr. Robert H. Anderson, project director for the Franklin

---

[3]S. E. Dean, "Team Teaching, A Review," *School Life*, XLIV, No. 1 (September, 1961), 5.
[4]"Though team teaching is new in a certain sense, it is actually an outgrowth of trends and movements in this and other centuries, rooted particularly in previous systems of deploying personnel and arranging pupils' daily programs." Robert H. Anderson, "Team Teaching," *Education Digest*, XXVI, No. 9 (May, 1961), 5. This article appeared in the NEA *Journal*, L (March, 1961), 52-54.

School experiment, eloquently describes this experiment by explaining: "We are questioning the *status quo*." The Harvard-Lexington Program has developed many of the distinguishing features of the team approach, which is now being used with variations throughout the country.[5]

The Claremont Graduate School, in Claremont, California, has successfully instituted teaching teams in many of the schools in Southern California. Aided by grants from the Ford Foundation Fund for the Advancement of Education the Claremont Plan has been expanded, and several California schools cooperatively with the Claremont Graduate School are now using a team teaching setup that amounts to "a school within a school." The Claremont Graduate School projects over the past three years represent some of the best team teaching efforts in the nation.[6]

Team Teaching Projects Across the Nation

There are also team teaching projects being carried out in Norwalk, Conn., Flint, Michigan, Evanston Township, Ill., Fort Wayne, Indiana, Wayland, Mass., Montgomery County, Maryland, Palo Alto, California, Pittsburgh, Pa., and Norridge, Illinois.[7] Ridgewood High School, at Norridge, Ill., is one of the few examples in which the entire high school is on a team teaching program. Naturally it would be impossible to describe all of the team teaching programs that are in progress throughout the nation,[8] nor is this necessary, since there are certain common features of team teaching which can be isolated and examined. The examination will take place later.

[5]The outlines of team teaching began to appear at Englewood, Florida, and Carson City, Mich., in 1956. The Franklin School in Lexington, Mass., began the first full-scale program one year later.

[6]See Azusa High School, Azusa, Cal. Other Claremont Graduate School team projects include Riverside, Fullerton, Palm Springs, Montebello, Upland, and other schools, all in Southern California.

[7]Not all schools have a sponsor, special funds or the impetus of a university research project. On the Norton, Mass., project see Wm. M. Mahoney, "Try Co-ordinate Teaching," *American School Board Journal*, CXXXIX (November, 1959), 13-14.

[8]There is now extant some excellent descriptive literature available, without charge, on many forms of team teaching. The Claremont Teaching Team Program — *Annual Reports*, are first-rate, authoritative guides on team teaching. See also the *1961 Annual Report, Pupils, Patterns, and Possibilities*, Superintendent of Schools, Pittsburgh, Pa. The latter is available without charge and is a comprehensive report on team teaching complete with drawings. On Ridgewood High School, the "team teaching" school, see Dorsey Baynham, "A School of the Future Operation," *Phi Delta Kappan*, XLII, No. 8 (May, 1961), 350-54.

Stimulus for Team Teaching

There is, however, a rapid evolutionary process going on. Perhaps the stimulus for team teaching comes from the fact that many schools in the present nuclear crisis are genuinely concerned with the improvement of instruction. In this respect team teaching would then be viewed as a plan for organizing a faculty for instruction, a form of "packaged cohesive learning." Many schools have been forced to consider changes due to burgeoning enrollments, and some simply for the sake of administrative convenience. Finally there is no doubt that many schools have jumped on the "team teaching bandwagon" because of the public relations value of educational change which they feel will give the semblance of improved instruction.

Change and American Education

In the past there has always been a time lag, often as long as 25 to 50 years, between the development of ideas and the institution of effective changes in school systems. In view of this fact, the great interest in and concerted action toward team teaching the past few years in many schools in the country is indeed remarkable. It reveals a sense of awareness about the problems which face American education, and also proves that educators do not fear change (as some claim) and feel secure in their eagerness to experiment.

Unfortunately, in their eagerness to experiment many educators have failed to recognize that there is no single approach or final answer to better education for the pupils of the nation's schools; much depends on the individual school's needs and situation.

The Bandwagon

Some schools are more or less stampeded into team teaching because "everybody seems to be doing it." R. N. Bush deplores this American proclivity of "jumping on the bandwagon" and facetiously says: "You are out of fashion this season if you have no experiment in team teaching or similar type of product."[9]

---

[9]Robert N. Bush, "Team Teaching Bandwagon," *California Journal of Secondary Education*, XXXV (April, 1960), 207-08.

Spurious Claims

One administrator argued that team teaching has had "quick success in the high schools of our country in the short space of seven years." Anyone familiar with team teaching projects knows that this is not a judicious statement, and this claim smacks of high infidelity. Team teaching must be properly understood. There are many forms and there is always a risk in innovation. Sometimes team teaching has to be tailored to suit the needs of a school, and serious consideration should be given the many variables involved in this approach to learning.

The history and facts of team teaching do not guarantee any "picture of success"; on the contrary, like any new idea, the teaching team concept can fail because of lack of understanding among those who try to use it. Here is an excellent recipe for those who would hastily improvise a teaching team delicacy without adequate support:

> The recipe is quite simple. Take an established, competent teacher, add two or more less ripened assistants, blend to form an integrated team and place in a conspicuous spot before a large group of youngsters. Then comes the period of watchful waiting. At this time we cannot evaluate the full impact of team teaching upon the pupils or, even, the individual members of the teaching group. Since this concept presents an exciting challenge to the schools, many administrators have embarked upon the team teaching program without sufficient introspection and adequate preparation. It seems that the key is to proceed slowly.[10]

Teacher Shortage

Since World War II every autumn has brought forth a new set of alarming statistics on the gap between teacher supply and demand. The best argument for the team plan is that maximum use is made of the teacher's abilities. However, a caveat must enter here. The team teaching idea calls for a willingness on the part of schools to discard the *status quo* of school organization: self-contained classrooms, egg-crate school houses, and the hallowed ratios.

---

[10]Milton E. Ploghoft, "Another Look at Team Teaching," *The Clearing House*, XXXVI, No. 1 (December, 1961), 219-221.

There is nothing sacred about the "old ways" of keeping school. James E. Allen, Jr., New York State Commissioner of Education, explains this well. In 1960 he wrote: "Never before in history have our schools engaged in such widespread experimentation to meet the new educational requirements. Never before have so many hopeful new approaches developed in such a relatively short period. . .In the process we are learning that many of the old ways of operating our schools are not necessarily the best ways."

Need for Proper Planning

Team teaching is no substitute for hard work and certainly is not a panacea for all educational ills. If it is not planned properly it could easily become a hollow form without any substance.[11] The recent results, however, are pointing us in a different direction and have guided us toward raising the quality of education. Instead of trying to meet the present emergency in orthodox ways by clinging to external forms and old conventional methods, schools should recognize that a new alternative exists — the teaching team idea.

Summary

We are entering a new era of science and technology and automation. Although the exact nature of these changes cannot be discerned, the resultant is bound to be a different social and cultural life with which education must deal.

Today more so than at any other time education has harnessed science to its help; however, regardless of the type of electronic aides used currently in American education and contemplated for tomorrow's schools the teacher is, and will continue to be, the "key figure" in our schools.

The accent on team teaching in recent years is due to the concern over teacher shortage, proper teacher utilization, and the advancement of methods of instruction. The basic concept of team teaching is not new, but its present application now tends to embrace new ideas on scheduling, curriculum, facilities, and diverse

---

[11]To guard against this the Claremont Plan provides a special training program in leadership and team procedures. The present correct title is the Claremont Graduate School and University Center.

groupings of students. This willingness to experiment will continue as change becomes part of the school's outlook. Many schools will find that the quick claims, the automatic success of team teaching, and the "bandwagon" approach are quicksilver foundations upon which to build a solid team teaching program. The old ways are not necessarily the best ways, and the new challenges offer new directions — and team teaching may be only one of these new paths.

Topics for Discussion and Study

1. Indicate the major economic, social and scientific changes which have had a great impact on American education since World War II.

2. Do social conditions today make fundamental readjustments desirable in our approach to learning? If so why?

3. What part does the burgeoning of scientific knowledge play in our search for new and better methods of instruction?

4. Describe the elements of change. Why has the attitude toward change in American education undergone a revision since the coming of the Cold War?

5. Select some problem in education today and show how a scientific approach has affected its solution.

6. Describe some of the new instruments and methods of learning which exist today that were not in existence in 1940. What part has science played in developing these new methods?

7. Why is team teaching a relatively old concept?

8. Why has team teaching, now being seriously reconsidered, become an important instrument for change?

9. Semantics plays an important part in the world of education. Explain why it is so difficult to define precisely such terms as "team teaching" and "flexible scheduling."

10. Do you think that experimentation in education will continue at the fast pace that it has since 1950? Why?

11. Draw up a statement of what you consider to be the most essential changes needed in the methods of instruction.

12. In what ways do you feel that team teaching could be advantageous in planning a curriculum which meets the needs of the individual student?

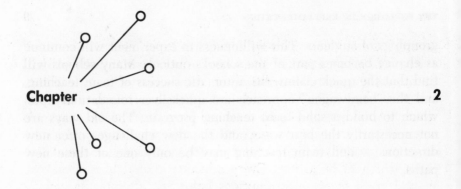

Chapter ——————————————————————————————— **2**

THE BASIC FRAMEWORK OF TEAM
TEACHING

Almost one hundred years ago James A. Garfield, the President of Williams College (1836-72), was satisfied with an educational situation which included a simple pine bench with Mark Hopkins sitting on one end and himself on the other. If President Garfield were alive today he would be amazed at the incorporation of administrative and technological changes and techniques which have filtered into the American educational system.

There is no doubt that he would find the modern organizational idea which we now call team teaching very puzzling. The educational institution of his age to a certain extent was isolated from the community, whereas the essence of team teaching is derived from an all-out determination to make meaningful use of everything and everyone in the school and community to add strength to the learning program, and thus via these community resources to extend the educational experiences.

No Fixed Formula for Team Teaching

This brings up the question: What are the basic assumptions behind team teaching? Some astute observers of the present American educational scene have taken a lukewarm attitude toward the teaching team concept. One writer warns: "The haunting dilemma which remains as of this date, however, is the lack of a sound philosophy to support the experimentation in team teaching."[1]

---

[1]Milton E. Ploghoft, "Another Look at Team Teaching," *The Clearing House*, XXXVI, No. 1 (December, 1961), 219.

Another writer differentiating between a "team" and a "non-team" stated: "In many so-called 'team enterprises' what actually exists is merely a voluntary federation of sovereign teachers. . .within which no one can be held accountable for performance of the program."[2] Although there is no universal formula for a teaching team since no two are likely to work in the same way, there are certain basic assumptions which should provide a philosophic foundation upon which to build one. Every educator should have some elemental grasp of these assumptions before he attempts to embark on a teaching team program. Unfortunately many educators do not have this and end up with some type of loose "flexible scheduling" which they call team teaching![3]

The basic assumptions of team teaching have one common element — they are pertinent on all levels of education from the elementary to the collegiate — that is if the prime purpose of education is to provide excellence in learning and instruction.

A Hierarchy of Teachers

Team teaching is based on the idea that talent is wasted, the teacher frustrated, and education watered down when all teachers, regardless of background and ability, are treated alike. These conditions could be improved by grouping teachers into teams, each led by a master teacher. Team teaching would then provide a necessary "hierarchy of teachers," with different levels of skill and competence and teachers paid accordingly.[4] Many team teaching projects avoid this phase of team teaching, going on the false premise that all the teachers are equal — something like George Orwell's *Animal Farm* where all in the barnyard were equal, however, some more equal than others! Already a serious shortage of highly educated manpower exists. This shortage will become increasingly critical unless we find enough of what the Ford Foundation calls the "seed corn" — teachers who, through their superior efforts which are well compensated, help to raise new generations of educated individuals.

---

[2]Robert H. Anderson, "Team Teaching," NEA *Journal*, I., No. 3 (March, 1961), 52-54.

[3]For lively and valid vignettes of team teaching see Arthur D. Morse's *Schools of Tomorrow — TODAY!* Commissioned and published in 1960 by the State Education Department of New York, Albany, New York.

[4]An excellent discussion of this issue is to be found in *Time, Talent and Teachers*, published by the Ford Foundation (June, 1960), 6-10.

The Claremont Plan for team teaching revolves around this concept. Because good teaching is an art of the highest order, we cannot hope to find a large number of teachers with first-rate ability. It therefore becomes necessary to seek ways of altering the teacher-pupil ratio without reducing the quality of education.

Proper Staff Utilization

Proper staff utilization and the prospect of attaining a superior position, with concomitant rewards, would likely attract more talented people to the profession, thus greatly aiding recruitment efforts.

Team teaching allows a group of teachers to pool their knowledge and talents in the instruction of a larger number of pupils than an individual teacher could normally handle alone. Many educators misunderstand this assumption. They go on the premise that two heads are better than one, and that the instruction of large groups will ease the administrative burden.

Self-Contained Classroom Questioned

Team teaching takes the teacher and his subject out of the isolation of the self-contained classroom and places him on a team which utilizes his talents and strengths. Team teaching facilitates grouping, not for convenience but to make instruction more effective. In other words just as teachers are "redeployed" pupils are "regrouped," depending on the subject being taught and the students' individual abilities. The key then to team teaching is the redeployment of personnel, pupils, salaries, and curriculum aided by a more flexible scheduling and adaptable physical facilities for instruction.

Team teaching saves time. It frees the teacher from the routine tasks (mostly clerical), permits him to plan carefully, and to keep up with numerous changes in his field. Inevitably this will improve the quality of his teaching and do wonders for his morale!

In-Service Training

One of the professional obligations which teachers have, as do members of other professions, is to assist in the training of new members of the profession. The teacher-in-training finds himself in an excellent in-service program when he becomes a part of a team. Here, under the protective wing of more experienced members of the profession, he can take active part in teaching by sharing the teaching load with the team members. Under the old isolated, self-contained classroom situation the teaching apprentice was often relegated to some form of pedagogical paper project which did little to improve his teaching talents.[5]

The Administrator and Team Teaching

It is possible that the teaching team could provide the administrator with a new unit, a type of unofficial "teaching cabinet" through which he could obtain suggestions for improving the curriculum and, in the final analysis, the general instructional program of the school. This, however, would depend on whether the administrator understands his role vis-à-vis the teaching team, and is quick to take advantage of this new instructional organization.

The Role of the Individual

Finally, one assumption which should not be overlooked is the impact that team teaching would have on the individual pupil. Flexibility in scheduling, proper grouping, the use of community resources, open vistas where the student can move as fast as his abilities carry him — all of these factors, plus the realization that the student is mainly responsible for his own education should indeed benefit him and bring an excitement to learning which is often lost in the "tell-and-test" classroom.

These assumptions would be valueless if they could not be effectively put into practice. The vehicle which carries these assumptions into action is the teaching team itself.

It is not easy to define a teaching team because teaching teams fit no one pattern. They are of various sizes and compositions. One thing is certain: much that passes for team teaching today is nothing more than departmental planning surrounded by overhead

---

[5]An excellent discussion of assumptions and possible teaching team models is to be found in the John A. Brownell and Harris A. Taylor article, "Theoretical Perspectives for Teaching Teams," *Phi Delta Kappan*, XLIII (January, 1962), 150-157. Mr. Taylor was director of the Team Teaching Program sponsored by the Claremont Graduate School and University Center, and Mr. Brownell is a member of the executive committee and edits program publications.

EDUCATIONAL OPPORTUNITIES*

one teacher per class limits

team teaching expands

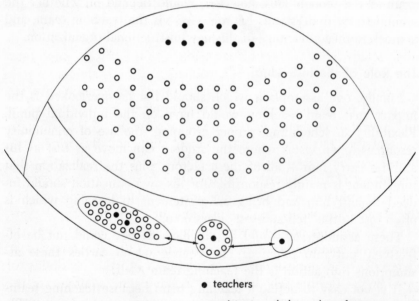

● teachers

● assistants—clerks, sub-professor

o students

*Extracted from J. L. Trump and D. Baynham, *Guide to Better Schools: Focus On Change* (Chicago, 1961), p. 22.

projectors! This kind of inadvisable planning puts one in mind of the statement made by Walter Kerr who when contemplating the purchase of a poor drama opined that it was the kind of play that gave failure a bad name! It was this type of poor planning which led one educator to answer in a team teaching survey that he hoped that "we would nail this heresy to the school house door!" Team teaching is not a heresy, and neither is it a toy for beleagured educators to play with and then hope for miraculous results.

Suggestions for Team Teaching Planning

If you contemplate teaching teams in your schools, here are several important topics or areas which should receive a major amount of attention: (1) the functioning of the teaching team — the training and selection of the members, their background and experience; (2) the method of selection, status, and proper compensation of the "lead" or master teacher; (3) the need for and scheduling of a planning period for the team; (4) the teacher-pupil ratio as it relates to the loads of other teachers and the traditions of your particular school; (5) the problem of scheduling students for the team and for regular courses and certain electives; (6) the nature and type of in-service education at your institution; (7) the implications of the "team" idea for the school staff, and the administration; (8) the selection and structuring of the small groups of students; (9) the quantity and quality of the peripheral services (such as guidance and counseling, etc.) available at present; (10) the sound approaches to the problem of good public relations; (11) the use and possible recruitment of "citizen aides"; (12) the amount of community resources available; (13) the mechanical, electronic, and optical devices available; (14) the possibility of providing a flexible schedule; (15) making time available in the school program to provide workshops in which to train team members; and finally (16) considering carefully the initial costs and relative expense of your teaching team plan.

Physical Facilities

Nothing has been said about the physical facilities because teaching team plans must be made commensurate with the physical facilities available — unless, of course you contemplate building a new school plant. This is not as farfetched as you may think, and many school districts have done just that.[6]

Structure of Teams

A teaching team can be structured at any level — elementary, secondary, junior college or a four-year college. Teams are usually concerned with one subject field, but their function and purpose sometimes take them across subject field lines. They all aim at one target — educational excellence!

The Role of the Gifted Teacher

Teams are usually structured "vertically" or "horizontally." Teams at all grade levels in a single subject or closely related subjects work vertically, whereas teams at one grade level, but in several subject areas, are horizontal teams. Teams usually have a "hierarchy of levels." In a sense team teaching carries into the schools the old principle of the division of labor. There is, however, a differentiation of roles. In general the team concept provides for the highly gifted teacher to be assisted by others, i.e., regular teachers, trainees, aides, etc., who perform the essential tasks so necessary when activities are coordinated.

The organization of teaching teams varies. The most popular arrangement seems to follow the master-teacher pattern. Here the master-teacher or team-leader accepts the responsibility for coordinating the team's efforts. He is accorded status and is usually paid a higher salary than the other members of the group.

The Team Leader

Many schools avoid giving the team leader any compensation, and fail to recognize that this is an excellent opportunity to give outstanding teachers the recognition they so rightfully deserve. The best advice on this matter is to be found in the Claremont Plan. The *Second Annual Report* advises that: "Each faculty team has

---

[6]For an excellent review of new schools built for the purpose of team teaching see Evans Clinchy, ed., *Schools for Team Teaching*, Educational Facilities Laboratories (February, 1961). Copies of this colorful booklet with its new architectural designs can be obtained from the office of the above, 477 Madison Avenue, N. Y. 22, N. Y.

an elected or appointed leader who accepts responsibility for co-ordinating his team's effort. He is paid a stipend above his normal pay for this responsibility. . .In the secondary school he is given an extra period, . . . to plan and coordinate team activities; in the elementary school he is relieved of teaching from time to time by an auxiliary teacher for the same purposes."[7] The master-teacher approach provides a new career line which did not exist in the traditional school.

The Associate Type Team

Another kind of team is the "associate" type which consists of several teachers joined together to form an instructional bloc. At the secondary level this two or three member team is usually ob-tained from one subject area and is a form of the departmental group project often used in the past. There is no leader as such in this type of team so the planning and instruction must be ham-mered out by the members of the team. If in team teaching there is the concept of "we" rather than "I" and the members of this leaderless team accept this, then the associate type team could be fairly successful; however, this leaves unsettled the matter of coordination and team responsibility.

Leadership and the Team

The "master teacher — beginning teacher" type of leadership is sometimes used to teach large groups. The relationships are, of course, fixed by traditions in the profession, and it would seem that this would be an excellent in-service situation. This type of team is not often utilized. It should be pointed out, however, that there is not one definite team organization that is more advan-tageous than another; much depends on the school's needs and particular situation.[8]

Coordinate teaching has not been included in this analysis of team teaching organization because it is primarily a "non-team" arrangement in which each teacher is responsible for his own class.

[7]See *Second Annual Report to the Ford Foundation by the Claremont Teaching Team Program for 1960-61*. Claremont Graduate School and University Center, 4.
[8]For an excellent discussion of various types of teams see L. L. Cunningham, "Team Teaching: Where Do We Stand?" *Administrator's Notebook*, VIII, No. 8 Univ. of Chicago, April, 1960), 1-4.

Although there is some co-operation and collaboration there are no assignments of specific leadership or responsibility. Team teaching means much more than simply throwing a group of teachers into close proximity!

The Composition of the Team

The team leader theoretically would have three to six colleagues, each representing a certain subject area. The team would have the same planning period every day. There would also be assigned to the team auxiliary personnel such as teacher aides, internes or auxiliary teachers, and laymen with special talents needed in the school program.

Teacher Aide

A very important part of the team is the teacher aide. One teaching-team member expressed it this way: "Take away my extra prep time, my new laboratory equipment, my overhead projector — just don't take away my aide!" In addition to doing the clerical work (typing, keeping records, attendance, etc.), the aide can perform the routine tasks of teaching which do so much to lower a teacher's morale and decrease his efficiency. Reference is made here to such time-consuming and often irritating tasks as giving make-up examinations, grading papers, and proctoring examinations. It would be easy to make too much of the "teacher aide" concept if it were not for the fact that educational literature is full of indictments against a system which vitiates a teacher's effectiveness by its continual "paper avalanche."

It is the teacher's aide who makes the plan that allows teachers to teach. Through the device of the aide the teacher can devote time to professional duties; he is free to plan and evaluate and to do creative teaching. Teachers are able to break through the "paper wall" which so often separates them from their students, and thus give pupils more individual help.[9] The aide is more than a clerk.

---

[9]"These nonprofessional tasks take a severe toll in time — from one-fifth to two-thirds of the teacher's day, according to a scientific time study of the elementary schools in Bay City, Mich., a few years ago." *Education: A Reappraisal,* published by the Fund for the Advancement of Education, New York, N. Y. See also The Yale-Fairfield Study of Elementary Teaching, Yale University, New Haven, Conn., for *Teacher Assistants: An Abridged Report.*

Many times the aide can assist the teacher in doing research on relevant instructional topics. There is also the possibility that because of the excellent on-the-job experience many aides may obtain the incentive to become professional teachers. Finally, when materials are prepared for the team these can be used by other instructional areas in the school. The teacher's aide thus benefits the entire educational program.

Interne Teacher

Some teaching teams use the auxiliary teacher or interne teacher as a part of the team. The service of the auxiliary teacher or interne gives flexibility to the schedule, and in the absence of a "teacher member" of the team provides continuity of instruction. This professional experience is much more valuable than the old practice teaching method. The necessity of planning closely with colleagues brings about an appreciation on the part of the members of the team of each other's knowledge and skill. Problems are shared in common, and the interne teacher soon acquires a group consciousness which is sometimes lacking in the old traditional method of teaching due to its situational isolationism.[10]

Electronics and Team Teaching

One of the important objectives of team teaching is to facilitate the learning situation through the maximum use of technological devices, equipment, and facilities. Many professional teachers are skilled in the use of projectors, tape recorders, and audio-visual equipment in general. What they need is the learning opportunities to utilize these properly; in other words to take advantage of the facilities both in the school and outside the school — in the community.

Use of Community Resources

We have heard a great deal in recent years about the use of community resources; however, it would not be unfair to say that

---

[10]On the pyramid or apprentice system of teaching see Richard W. Elliott, "Team Teaching Effective In-Service Training," *American School Board Journal*, CILIV, No. 2 (Februrary, 1962), 19; and *New Directions to Quality Education*, Commission on the Experimental Study of the Utilization of the Staff in the Secondary School, 200 Gregory Hall, Urbana, Illinois.

many teachers dip very lightly into the treasury of community resources. Team teaching provides the opportunity to bring into full
play not only the technological advances but also the various community resources. One excellent description of team teaching por-
trayed the use of these resources by pointing out that "talented
citizens, such as mathematicians, engineers, scientists, historians,
linguists, artists, musicians, help incorporate new developments
in the academic disciplines into high school courses."[11] In this way
the teacher's time and the community resources are aimed at one
target which results in cohesive learning with meaning. It is hoped
that through the proper use of the community's resources and in-
viting the citizen with talent to become a contributing member
of the school society not only will the horizon of the pupils be
broadened but, as a by-product, the school and the community
bonds will be strengthened.

Citizen Interest in New School Programs

Whenever we speak about community resources we usually have
in mind the resourceful citizen who has some special talent to contribute to the school's academic program. This is a rather shortsighted point of view. Many of our citizens who have specialized
talents are more than willing to help the school program, and their
aid should be welcomed. The teaching team concept should properly harness all the educational ideas and put these to good use.
In this way it will be possible to forge new weapons of precision
in education.

WORKSHOP AIDE AND TEAM TEACHING. An excellent example of this
approach is the "Instructional Aids Workshop," a program which
constructs aids for teachers and students in the Pomona, California, elementary schools. This is a Pomona Council PTA project
which has provided more than 363 instructional aids for the elementary classrooms. Two types of instructional aids are offered.
One includes items used by the teacher in instructing the class
(flannel boards, reading and speech aids, etc.). The second feat-

---

[11]See the excellent and descriptive booklet titled "The Claremont Teaching Team
Program: A Research Project," published by the Claremont Graduate School and
University Center, Claremont, Calif., 1961, 12. There is surprisingly little research
on team teaching and the use of the community's resources. Many valuable sug-
gestions are to be found in "Locus of Change: Staff Utilization Studies," *The
Bulletin* of the National Association of Secondary-School Principals (January, 1962).

ures aids, such as consonant boards, which the student can use without supervision by the teacher. The aides are available to any teacher in the Pomona Schools. The workshops were not organized as a money-saving effort, however, but as a PTA service program to free the teachers from time-consuming activities in preparing instructional aids. This is only one small example where the introduction of fresh ideas in education and the new methods by which to proceed have helped to improve our instructional program. The ferment caused by team teaching, the teaching machine, and programming have brought about a renaissance in educational thought.

Grouping and Team Teaching

No discussion of teaching team organization would be complete without some consideration of the necessity of grouping in team teaching and the innovations of school architecture to comply with the dictates of team teaching.

The short supply of teachers and the continuing pressure of higher enrollments were bound, in time, to bring about a reconsideration of class size. Many educators argue that the group of 100 to 150 will learn much easier in a lecture situation because it will help to develop individual responsibility on the part of the listener.[12] This is a plea for the development of independence on the part of the student. How the tide shifts — only a short time ago educators were deploring the "lecture method" with its concommitant faults, and now the rationalization, due in part to increased school costs, is based upon individual development! This is one of the weakest points in the armor of team teaching, and much consideration will have to be given to this phase of team teaching later. In other words — what are the human considerations of team teaching? What happens to young students when they are thrown into large groups in a lecture hall?[13] Some argue that even in small groups

---

[12]Will Hemeyer and Jean B. McGrew, "Big Ideas for Big Classes," *The School Review*, LXCIII, No. 3 (Autumn, 1960), 308-317. This article distinguishes between coordinate teaching and associate teaching and then goes on to describe the "big class" and the type of associate teaching used in the Rich Township High School, Park Forest, Ill.

[13]Judson T. Shaplin, "Team Teaching," *Saturday Review*, XLIV, No. 2 (May 20, 1961), 54-55, 70. This article discusses, in part, the potential pitfalls involved in this approach to instruction.

pupils do not gain any learning advantage. One writer wrote: "Unfortunately, teachers, when given the privilege of classes of fifteen or twenty, typically teach them about the same as if the classes were larger, and the research results, as conventionally measured, do not show significant gains in pupil knowledge of facts and principles."[14] If this is true then the size of the class does not, in the final analysis, really matter, but instead what really matters is the purpose of instruction. Since there is no magic in the standard class size of 25 or 30, then when background material is being presented the group could easily be over 100. With competent teachers in command instructional materials could be well presented, and then discussion groups would be formed. There is nothing novel about this type of instructional situation. It has been, and is being, undertaken in large universities throughout the nation.

Large-Group Instruction

At any rate, large-group instruction is a basic part of team teaching. It would not be feasible to commit five to seven teachers to a small group; and its costliness could bring about diminishing educational returns. In reality the large-group lecture sets the stage for team teaching. The purpose is presentation, and instead of the traditional five periods per week there probably would be only one to three, depending on the type of flexible scheduling provided (*infra*). This approach embodies efficient staff utilization since it saves the teacher's time and energy, allows him freedom to prepare his lectures properly, and keep himself up-to-date.

THE STUDENT AND LARGE-GROUP INSTRUCTION. Large-group instruction lends itself easily to a variety of teaching techniques, especially those which have been developed recently such as educational television. The student will find a greater interrelationship of ideas (if the material is presented properly), and will find himself in a position which will help him sharpen his sense of judgement in chosing important and significant facts for later study and review via continual and consistent note-taking. This should be of great value in his later education, and in a short time students learn

---

[14]Lloyd S. Michael, "New Directions to Quality Education in Secondary Schools," *The Bulletin* of the National Association of Secondary-School Principals, XLV, No. 261 (January, 1961), 13.

to accept the large-group arrangement. This is not to say that if he has difficulty in the group he is lost in a "sea of faces."

Counselors' Role in Team Teaching

If the team is properly constructed he will be able to obtain help from members of the team because the dichotomy between teaching and counseling will disappear. One writer placed emphasis on this when he wrote: "Actually counselors should be members of teaching teams. . .I have little faith in the kind of counseling that means talking to a student once or twice a semester in a 15-30 minute interview. Counselors need to work with teachers to observe pupil behavior."[15]

Facilities and Team Teaching

If team teaching emphasis is on the large-group lessons then buildings and their space should serve the needs of the students and the philosophy of instruction.[16] Too often school buildings reflect the *status quo* of traditional teaching and operational procedures of the staff. Unfortunately this limits the nature and kinds of activities than can go on in a school.

The New Classroom

If we support the belief that students can learn in large groups and in discussion groups then we must provide the atmosphere and space to accomplish this belief. Any area that is too small prohibits a pattern of collective activity, and any educator would indeed be foolish to attempt organized teaching and learning without giving some thought to the proper housing of this educational activity. The ordinary classroom is not suited to the team teaching

---

[15]J. Lloyd Trump, "Some Questions and Answers About Suggestions for Improving Staff Utilization," *The Bulletin* of the NASSP, XLV, No. 261 (January, 1961), 21.

[16]See "Flexible Classrooms for a Flexible Curriculum," *School Management*, III (November, 1959), 45-47, which discusses the architecture of the Carson City, Mich., Community School, where there is a team approach to learning. See also "Schools for Team Teaching: Profiles of Significant Schools," prepared by Evans Clinchy, by the Educational Facilities Laboratories, Inc., 477 Madison Ave., New York 22, N. Y., which includes drawings and floor plans of schools on all levels designed to house team teaching programs and provide the flexibility essential to a team approach.

activity, nor is the double classroom separated by the "cloth-type" room separator. This is not a soundproof situation, and too many educators have found this to be an "architectural delusion," unsuited for team teaching. The traditional school restricts the activities of the teaching team; what is needed for the building of tomorrow is "flexibility built into nearly every cubic inch."[17]

Plant Planning and the Team Plan

Architecturally, the teaching team makes demands on the school facilities which cannot be met simply by moving a few partitions. You do not obtain flexibility, expansibility, convertibility and versatility by a few innovations. Team teaching calls for "plant-planning." In the first place a large area is required for a minimum of a hundred students. This is the large lecture hall which can be equipped for easy blackout so that overhead projectors and slide and 16 mm film projectors can be used. Stand-by lunchrooms, although adaptable, are often inadequate. A part of the space segregation will have to be given over to separated areas for small groups and for discussion; these should be areas which serve to stimulate animated interchange of thought. Here we see that the school of the future has broken away from the "row of boxes" idea of the traditional school.[18] Other sections of the school should be planned for team teaching such as the library where the students can do self-directed research and an area for independent study carrels.

Future School Needs

The classroom shortage at the opening of the 1962-63 school year was 121,200, according to the U. S. Office of Education *Reports*. It is obvious that we will have to build many more schools to meet our present needs, and these buildings will have to incorporate the new and adventurous thinking which is necessary to

---

[17]S. E. Dean, "Team Teaching, A Review," School Life, XLIV, No. 1 (September, 1961), 7.
[18]An excellent and humorous layout for the future housing of team teaching can be seen in Bill Caudill's "The Case of the Busted Box," *New Schools for New Education*, Educational Facilities Laboratories, (New York City, N. Y.), 19-20.

meet the country's educational challenges.[19] We know now that the old "cells and bells" concept is outmoded. The architects of today stand ready to provide many innovations to suit the needs of the schools of tomorrow.[20]

The Dundee Program

This program has already been started. The Dundee Elementary School in Greenwich, Conn., for example, is one of the first schools specifically designed for team teaching. Before discussing the architectural innovations it is interesting to note that there are certain things the Dundee program is "not" doing. In the first place "it has *not* been set up to raise the student-teacher ratio nad help the school district save money. As a matter of fact the program — when fully operational — will cost about 15 per cent 'more' than normal."[21] The Dundee team teaching plan uses the "associate" type of team leadership (*supra*). The entire program is evaluated by a staff from Columbia University Teachers College financed by a Ford Grant; "it is *not* just a showcase for somebody's bright idea."[22]

Design for Team Teaching

The school's physical setup is the heart of the program. Specifically designed for team teaching, the split-level school is divided into three parts: a two-story section containing small-group areas, classrooms, and "team headquarters" for the teachers; a one-story section containing the library, school administration offices, and the large-group areas; and finally a one-story section housing the gymnasium-cafeteria and the service areas. Some of the special feat-

---

[19]See "A Place Out of Space . . . The Independent Study Carrel . . . and a Variety of Studies in Lakeview High School, Decatur, Ill.," by David W. Beggs and James L. Olivero, *The Bulletin*, NASSP, XLVI, No. 270, (January, 1962), 193-201.

[20]Englewood Elementary School, Englewood, Fla., Carson City Elementary School, Carson City, Mich., Lampere Public Schools, Madison Heights, Mich., Marie Creighton Junior High School, Jefferson City, Colo., are only a few of the schools, designed especially for team teaching. See Educational Facilities Laboratories *Reports, op. cit.*

[21]On the Dundee *Report* see Howard J. Langer, "Team Teaching at Dundee," *The Scholastic Teacher*, XXXIV, No. 5 (Feb. 27, 1963), 5 T.

[22]*Ibid.*, p. 5T. Many types of team teaching facilities are adequately described in Part II, "Locus of Change: Staff Utilization Studies," *The Bulletin*, NASSP, XLVI, No. 270 (January, 1962), *op. cit.*

ures which have been incorporated into this "team-teaching" building are: movable walls to expand or contract learning areas, small
rooms with tape equipment, complete wiring for television, a "talk-
back" intercom throughout the school, and a very unique idea,
Dundee's ten-channel audio system. This system is composed of
five tapes, three turntables, and two AM and FM radios. It is possible, via this system, to program into any room all ten channels
at one time. Each room contains forty outlets for earphones thus
making each of them a potential language laboratory. The description is only one of the many new team teaching plants now in
operation. It is still too early to analyze accurately the advantages
and disadvantages of the many new ideas which have been incorporated into the new school designs. One thing is certain: team
teaching programs operate under severe handicaps when forced
to function in the old traditional school building. The requirements
of team teaching are such that the educational barriers built in the
conventional plant must be removed. If you contemplate new
educational ideas then these new ideas must be properly housed.

Summary

One of the difficulties in modern education is that educational
semantics is not exact. Team teaching means many things, and
there is no fixed formula for a teaching team. There are some basic
assumptions that underwrite the concept of team teaching. For example, a solid team teaching program could feasibly be used to
provide a merit system in a school and provide a "hierarchy of
professional attainment."

Theoretically team teaching allows teachers to pool their knowledge, to utilize their strengths, save instructional time, provide for
in-service training, offer opportunity for new avenues for flexible
scheduling, and provide the administrator with a new staff structure.

A team teaching project should be planned with great care; every
phase of the school program and the facilities should be scrutinized before this planning begins.

The organization of teaching teams varies and teams are structured in various ways. It is suggested that the "team leader" con-

cept offers opportunity for professional advancement and provides the proper leadership for the team.

Team teaching invites the use of aides and the concommitant advantages which result from their use and provides an excellent opportunity for the interne teacher to prepare for a professional career.

Team teaching makes maximum use of the new technological devices and encourages the use of community resources. The use of electronic devices, however, will not insure the success of any team teaching program. Educators must carefully examine the present research regarding the grouping of students, methods of learning, and the impact of forms of instruction upon the individual student.

One thing is certain and it is that team teaching projects necessitate a willingness to discard old traditional ideas and to accept the challenge which experimentation offers. At present there is no formula for team teaching which will guarantee success; indeed team teaching is still in its incipient stage. Many educational questions will be raised during this experimentation; however, asking important questions in education often facilitates the search for solutions to important problems.

Topics for Discussion and Study

1. Why is it so difficult to define team teaching precisely?
2. Explain why some educators are attracted to the team teaching concept while many educators look upon team teaching as a simple staff relationship?
3. What are the basic assumptions of team teaching?
4. Discuss why you would tend to favor the "team-leader" or "master-teacher" approach or the "associate" type of team leadership.
5. List the advantages of team teaching which would improve student learning. What disadvantages would you consider as detrimental to a learning program?
6. If you intended to reorganize the school curriculum how would team teaching assist in this important improvement?
7. Draw a rough sketch of what you would consider a model teaching team (possibly for social science and English horizontal team).
8. Why do you think the aide would be of greater use and advantage for the team member than for the traditional teacher?

9. Explain how the new technological devices are an integral part of team teaching.

10. Team teaching offers a new possibility for the extensive use of community resources. Why?

11. Grouping, small and large, presents special problems for learning. Do you feel that team teaching could possibly provide a new answer to these problems?

12. What facilities are necessary for the success of a team teaching project?

13. If you were to list the architectural needs of a sound team teaching program what would you include in this list? Why?

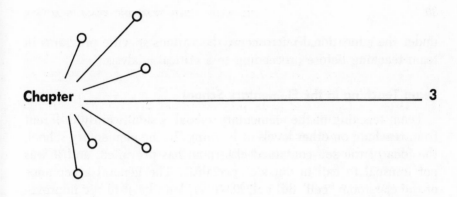

THE TEACHING TEAM IN ACTION

The literature on team teaching is full of glowing adjectives praising the multi-varied types of teams now in operation. It is only natural for each school to be proud of its "step toward change," but change simply for the sake of change is pointless. It would also be foolish to accept unquestioningly any idea that has worked well in one school as being appropriate for all other schools, or to import a few detached features of any organizational scheme and attempt to graft it on to your educational framework.

One staunch supporter of team teaching said with glee: ". . .I am convinced that when utilization of staff, space, and student capabilities is made to the fullest extent, then team teaching means 'quality education in quantity.'"[1] Not everyone is so completely convinced that team teaching means "quality education." Perhaps this element of suspicion is to some extent due to a lack of understanding of the team in action and a practical knowledge of what has been done in team teaching and the basic philosophy which underwrites it. It is only natural that programs which run counter to the conventional views will be subjected to extreme criticisms. Many of the criticisms have been general statements or observations, however; a more logical approach would be to examine,

---

[1]"New Horizons in Learning," _The Brevard County Project,_ Melbourne, Fla., 17.

under the educational microscope, the various specific programs in team teaching before proceeding to a critical analysis.[2]

Team Teaching in the Elementary School

Team teaching in the elementary school is significantly different from teaching on other levels of learning. In the elementary school, the idea of the self-contained classroom has prevailed, and it was not unusual to call in outside specialists. The general acceptance of the classroom "cell" did not, however, lend itself to the improvement of instruction. It was this element of isolation with its "eggcarton" construction, plus the necessity to attract into the profession accomplished teachers and retain them and to redeploy our teaching talents, that made the elementary school a fertile ground in which to plant the seeds of team teaching.

Models and Types of Teams in Action

One of the most successful elementary school team teaching projects is the Franklin School program in Lexington, Massachusetts. This program began in the fall of 1957.

Team Hierarchy Idea

Three teaching teams are used in the school with each team responsible for 150 to 180 pupils on two adjacent grade levels. The design of the team is a "hierarchy-of-teachers-pattern": there are three teachers, two senior leaders and a team leader. The roster of the team also includes three specialist teachers (art, music, and physical education) who provide instruction for pupils in all the groups. Members of the team, naturally, are the part-time teacher, interne, the teacher aide, and the clerical aide.[3] In this plan team leaders and senior teachers receive a salary supplement, and because they usually are career teachers there is a greater continuity in the over-all program. Here one finds the team teaching program placed on a sound basis, i.e., fully and properly supplied with per-

---

[2]See John I. Goodlad, "Experiment in Team Teaching," *Elementary School Journal,* LIX (October, 1958), 11-58; and John I. Goodlad and Robert H. Anderson, *The Nongraded Elementary School* (New York: Harcourt Brace & Co., 1959). The latter text argues the case for abandoning the graded school structure in the elementary school.

[3]See *Appendix B,* p. 126 on possible team model for elementary school.

sonnel who can promote the success of the instructional plan. It is most interesting to note that teams which have been successful have followed this model in general (there is no fixed pattern), and have used the "team hierarchy" approach. Schools which have left the leadership to drift in the amorphous cloud of group dynamics have been forced to admit later that friction developed during team operations.

The program uses flexible grouping and scheduling procedures based on the instructional needs of each pupil. It thus is possible to help each pupil to move at his own pace. The teams vary in size depending on the instructional purposes, and provision is made for independent study. Team teaching makes both extremes possible.

A "Scottish Clan" Approach to Team Teaching

A unique approach to team teaching is to be found at Dundee Elementary School in Greenwich, Connecticut. Here there are three major teaching teams, each of which has taken the name of a Scottish clan. About 240 students are in the Stewart Clan (K-2), the Fraser clan has 140 students (3-4 grades), and 140 students are in the MacKenzie clan (5-6 grades). There is a fourth clan, the Barclay clan, which consists of teaching specialists in music, art, foreign languages, and physical education, plus specialists in speech therapy and psychology.[4]

TEAM LEADER PROPERLY COMPENSATED. The instructional team has four to six teachers, and uses the team hierarchy of a team leader and a senior teacher; both are compensated for their special contribution to the team. The team leader receives $700 and the senior teacher $350 more than the regular teacher. The team also has a practice teacher and a teacher aide as integral parts of the team.

GROUPING AT DUNDEE. How does a team such as this function? For two afternoons the team plans the curriculum content and teaching approach. Together they share in the large and small

---

[4]Howard J. Langer, "Team Teaching at Dundee," *Scholastic Teacher*, XXXIV, No. 5 (February 27, 1963), 5-T-6-T, 10-T. There is a great deal of literature to be found on team teaching in the elementary school. See also P. Lambert, "Team Teaching for the Elementary School," *Educational Leadership*, XVIII (November, 1960), 85-8; and on the Franklin School see Alan Levensohn, "Team Teaching for the Elementary School," School Management, II (December, 1958), 45-48.

TRADITIONAL CLASSROOM PLAN
4 teachers, each with a class of
36 pupils (144 pupils)

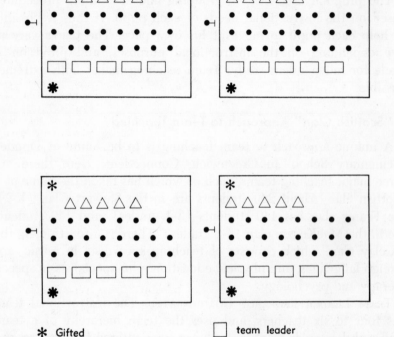

✳ Gifted	☐ team leader
△ Able college-going	⅃ Teacher
• average	ℰ Teacher Interne
☐ below average	
✳ slow	

To be found in "Pupils, Patterns, and Possibilities," 1961 Annual Report, Board of Education, Pittsburgh, Pa., p. 14.

TEAM TEACHING PLAN FOR A
THIRD-GRADE CLASS OF 144 PUPILS
IN THE PITTSBURGH PUBLIC SCHOOLS

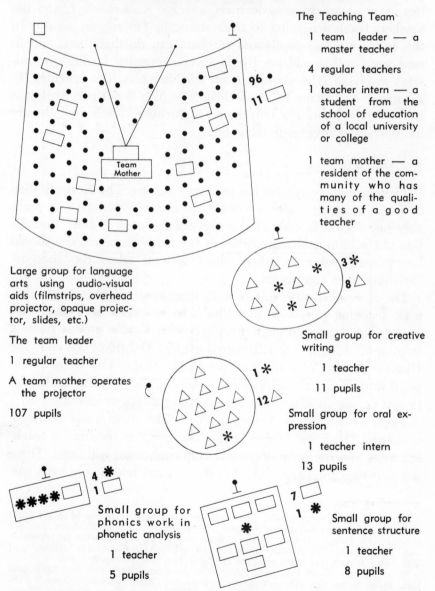

The Teaching Team

1 team leader — a master teacher

4 regular teachers

1 teacher intern — a student from the school of education of a local university or college

1 team mother — a resident of the community who has many of the qualities of a good teacher

Large group for language arts using audio-visual aids (filmstrips, overhead projector, opaque projector, slides, etc.)

The team leader

1 regular teacher

A team mother operates the projector

107 pupils

Small group for creative writing

1 teacher

11 pupils

Small group for oral expression

1 teacher intern

13 pupils

Small group for phonics work in phonetic analysis

1 teacher

5 pupils

Small group for sentence structure

1 teacher

8 pupils

Copied from "Pupils, Patterns and Possibilities: A Description of Team Teaching in Pittsburgh," *1961 Annual Report* of the Superintendent of Schools, Board of Education, Pittsburgh, Pa., p. 15.

group instruction. Only the language arts, reading, and math have homogeneous grouping; the remainder of the subjects have heterogeneous grouping. The pupils are divided according to their abilities (rapid learners, slow learners, average readers, etc.), and the teachers teach according to their strengths (in subject areas). In this way both the pupils and teachers can do their best, and in case any pupil should need help special remedial facilities are always available. The Dundee team teaching plan also provides for a home-room teacher for each child. The plan is not perfect, but it has been in operation only since September, 1962, and already has opened new vistas in education.[5]

The Norwalk Plan

There are many approaches to team teaching. The Norwalk Plan of Team Teaching is also one of the distinctive programs, and probably one of the largest, at the elementary level. A brief description of the unique characteristics of the Norwalk experience should be of some value to other school systems when they become "teaching team" conscious.

The Norwalk Plan is different, in some respects, than most other team teaching programs, and this is to be expected. Teams vary in size from three to eight members who handle groups ranging from seventy-five to two hundred pupils. Dr. Bryce Perkins, the Director of the Norwalk Plan points out that: "This is an adult-pupil ratio of one to twenty-five or less. . .The program is planned to cost no more and no less than the conventional program.[6]

TEAM STRUCTURE OF NORWALK PLAN. The structure of the team is simple. There are a team leader, one or more teachers, a teacher's aide, and the nonprofessional help each team will need. There is a part-time teacher attached to those teams which may have par-

---

[5]H. J. Langer, *op. cit.,* 10T. Many of the elementary team teaching programs are adequately described in the various project bulletins and publications. See, for example, *An Interim Report on the School and University Program for Research and Development 1957-1962,* published by SUPRAD, Cambridge, Mass., and *The Third Report, The Norwalk Plan of Team Teaching,* Norwalk, Conn.

[6]The Norwalk District is most helpful in describing their team teaching, and their bulletins are first-rate descriptive sources. See Bryce Perkins, "Team Teaching," *Educational Perspectives* (February, 1962), and Bryce Perkins, "Team Teaching," *The Instructor* (June, 1962). In the former article Dr. Perkins said: "The costs for a team-teaching approach are approximately the same as for a traditional program."

ticular need for one (such as remedial reading). The team leader is paid for his leadership responsibility. Also, after a year as a team member, each teacher receives $500 above the second step on the salary schedule. Once again we see a team hierarchy which is very successful.

THE UNGRADED APPROACH. The Norwalk approach is toward an ungraded situation in which two or more grades are combined and served by one team, and pupils are often grouped homogeneously unless they need remedial lessons. Tapes are used with work sheets, and pupils wear earphones to hear the teacher's voice clearly. The teams use all the audio-visual techniques that are available as an integral part of the team's program. All in all the Norwalk Plan is unique. It serves as an excellent model for school systems in the medium range of financial support in utilizing this instructional organization.

Elementary Level — Fruitful Team Teaching

The elementary level lends itself easily to team teaching for many reasons too obvious to mention. In one instance, for example, under the Claremont Teaching Team Program a whole elementary school was organized into three faculty teams with six to seven members. Even though team teaching does not fulfill all its promises it does challenge the traditional practices, and "they (teaching teams) will focus attention upon the need for improving the quality of teaching and counseling and for improving the use of the time and talents of teachers."[7]

The Junior High School

The junior high school was, and still is today to some extent, the transitory link between the elementary school and the high school. In spite of the fact that this most American institution attempts to develop a curriculum which will serve the growing child during his

---

[7]See *The Claremont Teaching Team Project: A Research Project,* Claremont Graduate School and University Center, 1961, 31. See also Dorsey Baynham, "Selected Staff Utilization Projects in California, Georgia, Colorado, Illinois, Michigan, and New York," *Focus on Change — The Bulletin,* NASSP, XLVI, No. 270 (January, 1962), 23. In 1961-62 the Claremont Teaching Team Program operated in nine school districts with 109 teachers and 3,352 students, and included twenty-one different teams with a variety of structures.

crucial years, there has been very little team teaching done on this level. The teaching team idea is rapidly spreading to other schools, and the problem now is not to start something new but to acquaint the junior high schools with the possibilities which team teaching offers in improving the quality of education.

Model Program

Only a few junior high schools have experimented with flexible programming and large-group teaching.[8] One possible model was the team teaching program started in New York City where three seventh-year classes in one large Manhattan junior high school developed a team teaching program in the area of reading. This area was chosen because the community from which students came contained many poor readers. It was a simple plan, begun in September, 1959. A lesson in basic reading skills was given each week to a group of about 120 pupils in the auditorium. A follow-up lesson was given another day by the teachers of these classes in the regular language arts room, and then later small-group instruction was provided for pupils who showed need for remedial study. A corrective reading teacher and one teacher with experience in reading at the elementary level served as demonstrators. Student teachers and new teachers were invited to observe the program and were given copies of the demonstrator's lesson plan of the large-group lessons. In this sense the teaching team was composed of the demonstrator (who gave the large-group lesson), the participating teachers, observing teachers, and student teachers. This plan is rather unique, and does not follow the more formalized pattern of team teaching composition.

Post Demonstration Conferences

Post demonstration conferences were held after each large-group lesson; evaluations and suggestions for improvement were made

---

[8]See D. H. Battrick, "How Do Team Teaching and Other Staff Utilization Practices Fit Into the Instructional Program of a Junior High School," *The Bulletin*, NASSP, XLVI (October, 1962), 13-15. For further suggestions see also G. A. Stetson and J. P. Harrison, "Junior High School Designed for Team Teaching," *American School* Board Journal, CXL (May, 1960), 38-42; and J. C. Stoltenberg, "Team Teaching in Junior High School," *Educational Leadership*, XVIII (December, 1960), 153-55.

at this time. The auditorium lessons covered a period of fifteen weeks, and in this time full use was made of effective audio-visual aids. During each lesson the pupils were given a skill sheet. The pupil was required to supply information and the work sheet acted as a guide for the demonstrator. This skill sheet served as an indicator of pupil weaknesses which could be corrected at the follow-up lesson period. Each pupil kept a notebook of the work covered in the large-group lesson.

Later, with the addition of three more schools, the program was expanded to the areas of mathematics and the language arts. Subject area specialists were then assigned to the team as resource personnel and curriculum assistants. Like many other experimental programs the junior high school experimental program in New York City left many questions unanswered. These questions are inherent, however, in any team teaching project, and should not deter any school from carefully experimenting in this direction.[9]

Claremont Project

The Claremont Project developed several junior high school programs which should be of great interest and benefit to educators attempting to improve instruction on that level. One of the teams at Chemawa Junior High School in Riverside, California, for example, provided large-group instruction in the social studies and English and small-group instruction in English and mathematics. The program included a laboratory day, scheduled three times a semester, to aid students deficient in any of the instructional area. As in other junior high school team teaching projects a developmental reading program was utilized in the English classes. The Eastmont Junior High School Team in Montebello, California, also used the laboratory approach to English (reading), geography, and mathematics. Interestingly enough, the Eastmont program correlated not only English and social studies, but also English and mathematics (spelling and vocabulary study), and social studies

---

[9]For a complete assay of the New York City Junior High Program see Joseph O. Loretan, "Team Teaching: Plus and Minus in New York City's Junior High Schools," *The Bulletin*, NASSP, XLVI, No. 270 (January, 1962), 135-140. An excellent source of accurate and varied team teaching programs can be found in *The Claremont Team Teaching Program, Annual Report 1961-62*, Claremont Graduate School and University Center, 1962, 8-15.

and mathematics (time lines and flag drawings). It was a part of team planning at both schools to make wide use of resource persons.

Use of Community Resources

The junior high schools took cognizance of community talent and brought into the learning situation engineers, stockbrokers, professors, scientists, authors, and even a fire inspector. Although the educational literature speaks fervently for the use of community resources it should be obvious that much depends upon the type of community in which the school is located. There is no magic to the phrase "community resources" unless the community in reality possesses these resources. Many educators automatically assume these community talents exist, which is not often the case. Before such a program is put into effect a careful survey therefore should be made of the community and its environs.

An example of very distinctive and unique use of community resources was the Chemawa Junior High Team. The Team organized fifteen two-hour evening meetings for small-group instruction in astronomy. All instruction was given by the President of the Riverside Astronomy Club.

Appraisal of Types of Team Teaching

There are many types and forms of teaching teams, and the possibilities are limited only by the imagination and the school facilities. None of these teams can be guaranteed to be completely successful, and it is still much too early in our experimental stage to be able to foresee the many pitfalls of any plan. It will be necessary to face up honestly to any difficulties which may arise during the operation of the teaching team. Only by an open diagnostic attitude can any improvement be made. A fine example of this is the honest appraisal made by the participants of the Claremont Plan. In regard to two junior high school programs, the *Annual Report* stated: "Inspection of the Chemwa and Eastmont teams' diagrams reveals that, because of scheduling programs, the teams did not have an uninterrupted block of time at their disposal. Such a condition reduces opportunities for developing cohesiveness, flexible grouping, and other instructional advantages."[10]

The Departure From Tradition

Any departure from tradition is certain to present difficulties and criticism. It would be foolish indeed to seek the answer to educational ailments in some form of inactivity or reaction. Experiments in team teaching on one level alone will not provide a satisfactory model for all grades of learning; the matter is too complex for such a simple solution. Experimentation all along the line will bring experiential guidelines that will lead to quality education.

The High School and Team Teaching

When Vittorino da Feltre (1378-1446), the "first modern schoolmaster," opened his school for youth in Mantua, Italy, he chose his pupils by their talent and eagerness to learn. He expected hard work from them and maintained strict discipline. His school represented a continuation of the Greek ideal, and became the model of some of the great classical schools of more recent times. Obviously da Feltre's school served a limited clientele, and would not be suitable for the needs of a democracy in a nuclear age even though his expectations were admirable. The last twenty years have seen vast sweeping changes in the conception of the role of the American high school.

Although change does not always imply progress, the American schools in the past decade have plunged willingly into new programs, experimented with new concepts and embraced new methods of instruction in the high hope that education could meet the challenge of the age. The American schools now face toward the future. Team teaching in the high school is the transitory link for the preparation of the future high school. In the specific, this new idea could furnish an impetus to significant curriculum improvement. It would be foolish, however, to expect major gains in curriculum and instruction to result automatically from some simple

---

[10]*Ibid.,* 8. A very fine article full of suggestions for the junior high school is P. B. Glancy, "Brookside Junior High School, Sarasota, Florida, Strives for Quality Education," *The Bulletin,* NASSP, XLVI (January, 1962), 157-60.

rearrangement in school organization, and much remains to be done in training personnel for leadership roles and devising efficient procedures for team operation.

A Multitude of Plans

Many schools have been attracted by the stimulating alternatives which team teaching offers.[11] Many plans blanket the nation and are too numerous to describe in detail. Fortunately, adequate and comprehensive descriptions of teaching teams on the secondary level are to be found in the current educational literature.[12] It would be advantageous, however, to sample some of the outstanding features of a number of the important secondary team teaching projects.

Bertrand Russell once argued that mathematics is "the subject in which we never know what we are talking about, nor whether what we are saying is true." In any analysis of team teaching an examination of the specific details of a team structure and its operational procedure will, in most cases, provide a clear and truthful picture of that particular team teaching program.[13] It is fruitless to deal in generalities.

The Wayland Plan

One of the most publicized secondary team teaching plans is the Wayland High School Plan in Wayland, Massachusetts. It is an organizational plan which divides the faculty into six teams on a "vertical" layout, i.e., each team contains all the instructors in a specific subject — all the mathematics teachers in one team, English teachers in another, etc. There is the typical team leader who is responsible for the planning, co-ordinating and leading of the team. The electronic sorters have scheduled the students so there is the large-group lesson, the small group or seminar type meeting, and

[11]"Right now, a full one quarter of all U. S. junior and senior high schools are trying out some form of team teaching." "The Platoon System of Teaching," *Life Magazine*, LIV, No. 12 (March 22, 1963), 79.

[12]See Nicholas C. Polos, "The Teaching Team in Action," *Journal of Secondary Education*, XXXVI, No. 7 (November, 1961), 415-19.

[13]For a very interesting project which offers many unique and challenging suggestions see *The Accordion Plan: The Pursuit of Excellence in the Weston Public Schools*, New England School Development Council, Cambridge, Mass., (February, 1960), 1-43.

classes of various sizes meet at different times. The students often have different teachers (depending on the latters' strength), and they are frequently grouped together according to ability. In this way teaching assignments are tailored to pupils whose needs have been carefully defined. One astute observer of this project wrote: "These arrangements for instructional groups form the basic plays from which there are many options. The schedule makes use of the concept of a week's instruction in contrast to a daily schedule. Instructional groups do not necessarily meet every day or at least at the same hour each day."[14]

For the three years it has been in operation, the Wayland project has wrestled with the one big problem which team teaching creates — the proper scheduling of students — but it hopes soon to overcome this problem by the use of the computer at Massachusetts Institute of Technology.[15]

PLANNED VARIABILITY. Wayland High School has one unique advantage which the older, traditionally built schools lack. It is an architectural advantage which has been called "planned variability." In describing the Wayland plant John C. Harkness (Architects' Collaborative, Cambridge, Mass.) wrote: "Planned variability characterizes the 'collegiate' design of this new high school in Wayland, Mass. A campus of six interlocking buildings includes academic centers for arts, sciences, languages and social sciences each staffed by a teacher team."[16]

The enthusiastic participants of the Wayland team teaching instructional program are earnestly striving to "take the boredom out of education." Surprisingly they argue that this is not a costly venture and that their project costs no more than the traditional program.[17] Here is a team teaching school that is worth watching!

The Ridgewood Plan

Another team teaching project which has challenged every traditional method of teaching is the program at Ridgewood High School

---

[14]William M. Griffin, "Some Ideas and New Patterns at Wayland, Massachusetts, High School," *The Bulletin*, NASSP, XLVI (January, 1962), 123-126.
[15]"The Platoon System of Teaching," *Life Magazine, op. cit.*, 82.
[16]Edward Anderson (Superintendent) and John C. Harkness, "Planned Variability," *The Nation's Schools*, LXV, No. 4 (April, 1960), 81.
[17]"Team teaching requires no more faculty than a conventional school, and it need cost no more." "The Platoon System of Teaching," *Life Magazizne, op. cit.*, 82.

at Norridge, Illinois. Many articles have been written describing the Ridgewood program which is unique in that it was especially designed both architecturally and organizationally to embrace the basic principles of team teaching. *Time* Magazine wrote that this program had "an air of concentration and the spirit of inquiry," and it is indeed a program which is worth examination by any school entertaining the idea of team teaching.[18]

The team teaching programs at Wayland High School and Ridgewood High School represent team teaching in "totality," i.e., team teaching organized throughout the entire school.[19] Many schools in the nation are not prepared, however, for such an "all out" offensive. A knowledge of various team teaching programs therefore is necessary so that the experience of many schools can be shared.

Representative Teams

At the secondary level there are several representative types of teams with only small variations. A detailed description of these can be easily obtained by writing to the various schools. These schools are only too eager to share their experiences with other educators.

°Evanston Township High School, for example, is organized on a schools-within-a-school plan, with four separate divisions. Teachers, however, are not divided among the four divisions but teach school-wide courses. The school's teams plan together, coordinating whole courses of study in various subjects.

°At the older *Newton High School* and the new *Newton South High School*, there are subject matter teams and teams made up of entire staffs of the separate schools-within-a-school, or "house," plan under which these high schools operate. One of the earliest to enter team teaching, Newton High School organizes the class size on the basis of the subject taught; these classes may range from 50 to 200 pupils.[20]

---

[18] The materials supplied by the Ridgewood High School are excellent. J. L. Trump, *Guide to Better Schools*, describes Ridgewood as one of the twenty-seven significant schools.

[19] A recent publication of the Educational Facilities Laboratories (Ford Foundation), entitled *Profiles of Significant Schools — High Schools 1962*, devotes several pages to detailed descriptions of Ridgewood and other schools which are carrying on important programs.

[20] See Henry S. Bissex, "Newton Plan Challenges Traditions of Class Size," *The Nation's Schools*, LXV, No. 3 (March, 1960), 61-64. For more recent detailed results and pertinent team teaching suggestions see "Locus of Change: Staff Utilization Studies," *The Bulletin* of the National Association of Secondary-School Principals, XLVI, No. 270 (January, 1962).

Easton Area High School, Easton, Pa., provides team teaching instruction in three academic subjects — English, history, and mathematics — within a four period block of time. Easton has an eight-period day, and the 1,800-pupil school program provides for large class sessions with about 90 pupils in a group. The program at Easton is unique in that it features a "tutorial phase," and two college-level seminars in English and history for selected seniors.

Verdugo Hills High School, Tujunga, California, developed a team teaching program with split week courses in order to make the program more flexible and develop electives. Although there were some disadvantages, on the whole the Verdugo experiment suggests that split-week courses are of great value to small high schools.[21]

The Hurricane High School Project at Hurricane, Utah, was constructed primarily to improve the Language Arts program in grades ten, eleven, and twelve. This program is described as an "ungraded English project," in which students are grouped homogeneously according to ability and skill in language arts and not according to grade levels. The program has many unique features and is worth examining carefully. Another team teaching program based on students' reading ability is the program at *McClymonds High School* in Oakland, California. Here students are grouped in certain of the fundamental academic subjects according to their reading age or grade.

It would be impossible to describe all the various team teaching programs that are now in progress. It furthermore is not necessary to do this; the important reason for scrutinizing the various team teaching programs is to obtain a comprehensive grasp of the underlying concepts of team teaching. Armed with this basic understanding of the teaching team it is possible to extend team teaching to more and more subject areas. It has been found to be effective in music, industrial arts, and even physical education.[22]

Different Approaches to Team Teaching

There are some different conceptions and interpretations of team teaching. The conception of the team, for example, in the Claremont Plan differs from that which guides most other teams, and their

[21]Gjertrud Smith, "Verdugo Hills High School, Tujunga, California, Introduces Split-Week Courses and Team Teaching to Add Flexibility to the Program," *The Bulletin* of the National Association of Secondary-School Principals, XLVI, No. 270 (January, 1962), 173-184.
[22]See *Bibliography,* p. 130 ff., for team teaching in various subject areas.

experiments, in the United States. In the main, a Claremont Teaching Team is an instructional unit within a school. This unit is a combination of a distinct student group; in secondary schools, 90 to 180 students who have chosen a similar program of courses would be a student team; and in the elementary schools, 150 to 200 pupils of particular ages or grades constitute a team.[23] The plan also calls for a small faculty group (three to six teachers who have the same conference period each day) with complementary talents and specializations to be responsible for the academic and counseling program of the student group, as well as for certain auxiliary personnel who assist in the instructional program. Block scheduling of team students (*supra*) and teachers permits variations in the length and sequence of classes. Such is the essence of the plan. When the scheme of organization is expanded to its utmost, a large high school of 2,000 students could conceivably be a cluster of fourteen teams covering the entire student body and faculty. The project, "The Claremont Teaching-Team Program," discusses the possibility of obtaining the greatest flexibility in both large and small high schools. Another aspect of the Claremont Plan (*infra*) is, of course, the use of "citizen volunteers" to enrich the instructional program. Schools in nine California districts have been testing the Claremont hypotheses.

The Fremont Plan

A typical team teaching project which involves two teaching teams (four teachers in social sciences and a team of two teachers in physical sciences) is in progress at Fremont High School, Sunnyvale, California. This high school has been experimenting with team teaching for over four years. The plan involves the typical use of teacher aides, audio-visual equipment (including a projecto-printer for many transparencies), and flexible planning. The four-member social science team plans twelve lecture sessions weekly which involves 540 students.[24] The large lecture classes are held

---

[23]On the Claremont Plan see Nicholas C. Polos, "Progress in Teacher Education — The Claremont Plan," *The Journal of Teacher Education*, XI, No. 3 (September, 1960), 398-401.

[24]See *Appendix B*, p. 126 for a comparison of the Teacher and the Pupil, the team and non-team.

each morning for both teams, with 90 students in a Senior Problems class and 120 students in Science I. The latter group meets in the lecture hall five days per week and biology classes two days per week while the 90-member social science group is subdivided on an average of once a week into six groups of 15. This arrangement is not too difficult to schedule. Fremont has been most enthusiastic about their program and is planning to expand it.[25]

Experimentation in One Subject Area

Those who are cautious would do best to experiment with team teaching in one subject area and on one grade level. A fine example of this type of experimentation is the social science team teaching program at John A. Johnson High School in St. Paul, Minnesota. This high school organized two experimental classes in 1959-60, one of 105 students in the twelfth grade Social Problems under the aegis of three experienced teachers, and one of 80 students in eleventh grade American History under three qualified teachers.[26] After some experimentation it was found that it would be advantageous if the twelfth grade group met in the auditorium for three days a week for the large group classes and the eleventh grade team used the auditorium the other two days. In order to make maximum use of space and facilities the small group meetings for both teams were held on the alternate days when not convening in the auditorium.

This is an excellent incipient approach to team teaching experimentation which will give any school experience that can serve as a foundation upon which to build other teaching teams that can encompass many subject areas.

College Team Teaching

Almost a century ago President Charles W. Eliot of Harvard broke the hold of the classical curriculum when he introduced the

[25]On the Fremont Program see Collins T. Haan and Roger C. Adams, "Experimentation at Fremont High School," *Journal of Education*, XXXVII, No. 5 (May, 1962), 274-279. See Also Dorsey Baynham, "Selected Staff Utilization Projects in California, Georgia, Colorado, Illinois, Michigan, and New York," *The Bulletin*, NASSP, LVI, (January, 1962), 18-19.

[26]On the Johnson program see *A Report On Team Teaching in the Social Studies*, Office of Secondary and Vocational Education, Saint Paul, Minnesota, August, 1961, 1-5; and Glenn F. Varner, "Team Teaching in Johnson High School, St. Paul, Minn.," *The Bulletin*, NASSP, XLVI (January, 1962), 161-166.

elective system. The rapid development of new knowledge called for the revolution he started. The vast extension of knowledge which provided the basis for the new technological society resulted in the addition of new subjects to the traditional offerings. American society today is rapidly becoming more complex, more technical, and requiring a higher level of formal schooling for its citizens. These factors plus the population explosion have placed a heavy strain upon college and university facilities. Colleges do not enjoy favored positions for they too are plagued with the problems which disturb the elementary and secondary schools. Inevitably most colleges are faced with increased enrollments and a shortage of good teachers, and some with financial difficulties due to rising costs.

As college enrollments soared it was obvious to all educators that unless facilities kept pace with the expanding student population the quality of education was bound to suffer. The college professor who was not burdened by the paraphenalia of obligations of the public school system (record-keeping, collecting milk money, etc.), and who like Chaucer's clerk of Oxenford was only too willing to admit that "gladly wolde he learne, and gladly teche," found himself engulfed by a sea of students!

Advantages in College for Teaming

A part of the attempted solution was to hold larger and larger classes which could later be broken down into smaller discussion groups. Colleges, unlike the secondary and elementary schools, had a decided advantage. In the first place they were not strangers to team teaching (although it was not called team teaching); second, the time blocks have, as a rule, been fairly flexible and not frozen into a pattern, and third, professors have been able to develop and teach in the areas in which they were best prepared.

HUMANITIES AND TEAM TEACHING. An excellent example of this is the Humanities Program at Scripps College in Claremont, California. The central feature of the curriculum is the sequence of courses in the two-year Humanities Program ("The Ancient World to America in the Contemporary World") given by the staff. This unusual organization of the curriculum brings together five broad fields of interest: literature; the arts; social studies; psychology, philosophy, religion; and science. This type of curriculum organization makes possible "an appreciation of the continuity and wholeness of learning." It is taught by highly trained faculty members forming a team. The courses are organized as seminars, and the objective is to help the student to develop independent study habits and "cultural self-understanding." This form of "core" program is not new, and is a program which the college pioneered many years ago.[27]

Collegiate Experiments with Team Teaching

In 1956 the Ford Foundation and the Fund for the Advancement of Education under a program by the Committee on Utilization of College Teaching Resources[28] began a series of experiments to "demonstrate a series of comprehensive approaches to general education."

Some of these experiments have been conducted at Austin College, Sherman, Texas; Wayne State University (a new division called Monteith College), Detroit, Michigan; Hofstra College, Hempstead, New York; Goddard College, Plainfield, Vermont; Antioch College, Yellow Springs, Ohio; and at the University of Kentucky. Using team teaching in various ways these collegiate institutions have attempted to revise their respective curriculums; promote independent study; provide large-group instruction; and bring into college instruction a wider use of modern audio-visual equipment and techniques.

*Austin College, Sherman, Texas — This program is in a sense similar to the older Scripps program. It is a two-year sequence of courses in the humanities and the natural sciences (history, philosophy, religion, literature, art, political science, psychology, sociology, and economics; the sciences included mathematics, physics and astronomy in the first year, and chemistry, biology, and geology in the second year). In beginning chemistry instruction is provided by the "Continental Classroom," the nationwide television course.

The program is called Basic Integrated Studies and involves about fifty-two freshmen and sophomores. The curriculum is organized

[27]On this program see The Scripps College Bulletin, 1962-1963, Scripps College, Member of the Associated Colleges, Claremont, Calif., 24-27.
[28]A summary report by the Committee, Better Utilization of College Teaching Resources (May, 1959), is available from the Fund for the Advancement of Education, 477 Madison Avenue, New York, N. Y.

by faculty teams; the members of the teams cross departmental lines in order to provide a "relevancy of knowledge."[29]

Many junior colleges and small four-year colleges would do well to investigate the experiment at Monteith College (approximate enrollment 1,100 students).

Monteith College (a division of Wayne State University, Detroit, Michigan) — This program uses the large-group lecture method (auditorium), as do many universities, coupled with the small discussion group procedure. The curriculum, however, is unique in that it centers around a sequence of related courses which describe man as a social being, as an artist, and his place in the natural world. Except for the engineering students, all students take four semesters of natural science, three of social science, and three in the humanities. The senior year involves a "colloquium," a form of discussion-group course where the student works more or less independently, and does his own reading. This new program in general education involves careful faculty planning; oftentimes instructional materials must be specially written for the new courses.

Hofstra College, Hempstead, New York — This curriculum, taught cooperatively by teachers from many fields, also emphasizes a core instruction in science and the humanities. An instructor gives the large-group morning lectures and these are followed by discusion groups led by the students. The program is scheduled on a four-day week since many of the students are employed part-time. The program is planned as a two-year experimental college.

Goddard College, Plainfield, Vermont — This program emphasizes student independent learning and offers broad fields of knowledge. Operating on a twelve-month school year, the students spend two months a year off the campus working on projects related to their academic interests. For example, it is possible to combine anthropology with the study of a language, and a student could spend his two months in the country of his language study. The emphasis is on self-directed study and the student project. Part of the Goddard Program is the extensive use of the Learning Aids Center, an audio-visual aid center, which is open to all students.

Antioch College, Yellow Springs, Ohio — One of the outstanding features of this program is the use of student teams to help other students. These frequently are utilized, for example, where students

---

[29]For a more detailed description of these programs see "College Teaching," *Time, Talent, and Teachers,* The Ford Foundation, New York 22, N. Y., 39-49. Further information can be obtained by writing to the Ford Foundation, Office of Reports, 477 Madison Avenue, New York 22, N. Y.

lead discussion groups. This college is famous for its part-time work program which is integrated into its curriculum.[30]

A New Approach to Teaching Mathematics

A very unique program for teaching large numbers of students in one subject area has been devised by the mathematics department at the University of Kentucky. Charged with the instruction of 4,000 students in mathematics, Kentucky with its ten full-time mathematics faculty members and small group of graduate assistants has been forced to take a long look at proper teacher utilization. The plan which the University devised is fairly simple, but effective. The senior faculty members teach all the large classes (approximately 360 students) in the basic courses. Because mathematics require individual help the plan uses the special "study room" arrangement where professors or graduate assistants give student help five days a week. The students thus are encouraged to work independently and also have access to competent instruction.

In using team teaching there is always the danger of oversimplification, brought about by the "halo" effect of a new program. There are many pitfalls in team teaching, and sailing the uncharted seas of new instructional programs is dangerous. To go off in all four directions at once, like Stephen Leacock's horseman, is a form of "curriculum madness." It is time to examine the pitfalls of team teaching critically.

Summary

Team teaching has found a fertile ground in which to plant its seeds — that area is the elementary school. The Franklin School program, the Dundee Elementary School program, the Norwalk Plan, and many other projects in team teaching on the elementary level have challenged the traditional practices of keeping school.

There has been little experimentation in team teaching on the junior high school level. Some of the projects have, however,

---

[30]*Ibid.,* 40-46.

*See *A Second Annual Report to the Ford Foundation on Team Teaching in Maine* (Orono, Maine: University of Maine, 1964) which describes an excellent college program in team teaching in their College of Education and in the public schools of Maine.

pioneered new ideas (remedial reading programs) in the use of community resources, flexible scheduling and grouping.

Many schools have been attracted by the stimulating alternatives offered by team teaching. The literature adequately describes the many projects which are in progress in the high schools across the nation. It would be impossible to recount all the various team teaching programs now in progress, nor is this necessary. A survey of the literature will assist the student of education to obtain a comprehensive grasp of the basic underlying ideas of team teaching.

There are many different conceptions and interpretations of team teaching. Many educators who have experimented with teaching teams agree on a central theme: team teaching offers many possibilities for the development of a professional hierarchy — a ladder for the advancement of teachers and a seedbed for professional improvement.

Team teaching has found its way into the American college. Although there have been only a few important experiments these projects show promise for the future expansion of team programs.

In any "step toward change" there is always the possibility of a program's acquiring a "halo" effect. The results of any team teaching project should be examined critically but not with hostility, since it is only natural that programs that run counter to the conventional views will be subject to emotional judgements.

Topics for Discussion and Study

1. How would you prove that team teaching does not necessarily result in "quality education"?
2. Discuss the factors that you think theoretically would make for a successful teaching team. What would be your criteria for making this judgement?
3. Why do you think that team teaching programs and this type of ex-- perimentation have been most extensive on the elementary level?
4. Do you agree that the team leader should be compensated for this leadership obligation?
5. Draw a rough outline of a sound teaching team on the elementary level, the junior high school level, and the high school level. This should be a "vertical" team with all of the team appurtenances.
6. Make a list of the many areas and combination of areas that could profit instructionally via the use of a teaching team.

7. Why is the use of "community resources," although valuable in assisting our educational programs, often exaggerated?

8. Explain the important relation between the manipulation of school time and the teaching team.

9. Describe the part that school architecture plays in establishing the teaching team.

10. Do you think that the "schools-within-a school" plan concept really influences individual learning in any way? If so how?

11. How would you employ audio-visual equipment to improve the teaching team?

12. What are the disadvantages of large-group instruction in a lecture situation in a large auditorium?

13. Describe a sound team teaching plan for a social science or humanities program in a college.

14. What is the meaning of "planned variability"?

15. Describe how you would measure the ultimate results of a teaching team in the social sciences and English.

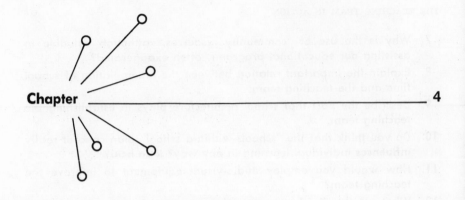

Chapter —————————————————————————— **4**

THE PITFALLS OF TEAM TEACHING

This is a time when we urgently need research and experimentation in education, however, resistance to change is built into our educational practices. Many educators fear change because of the difficulties, foreseen or unforeseen, which they might encounter. Many of these lack what David Riesman calls "the nerve of failure," and often refuse to face up to the shortcomings of any program but prefer to quietly bury it under some isolated educational rug. There are as many attitudes as there are educators, ranging all the way from the "time is not ripe" educator to the "hollow imitator for publicity purposes" educator. Somewhere in the middle of this range is the judicious educator who has carefully weighed all the possibilities and proceeds with intelligent action. He is aware of Edgar Dale's statement in the Ohio State Newsletter (December, 1960) that says: "But it is the weak man, not the strong man who wants absolute certainty. It is the essence of leadership not only to live successfully with uncertainty, but also to be challenged by it. . . ."

The common-sense educator recognizes that any departure from tradition will have its pitfalls, and he does not "play ostrich-in-the-sand" but attempts to steer his educational bark between Scylla and Charybdis skillfully.

The Bandwagon Appeal

Many of the surveys which we have conducted reveal, more or less, a great deal of enthusiasm for team teaching which appears to be superficial. The argument seems to run something like this: "Now this is the thing that is being done today, and why are you a 'doubting Thomas'?" In an excellent analysis of team teaching the authors entered this caveat by saying: "Because team teaching has a certain logical appeal and, at least in the present climate, an arresting glamour, there is now a real danger that some enterprising administrators will jump on the teaching bandwagon to the ultimate sorrow of the profession."[1]

Disadvantages of Team Teaching

Although many will disagree with this there are numerous fundamental questions which remain unanswered and there are many pitfalls in team teaching. These pitfalls are not simply the disadvantages which follow as a result of poor team teaching, but are obstacles in the road toward improving instruction which must be avoided. Some of these do not seem to be directly related to good team teaching practices but they influence the ultimate result.

Here in brief summary are some of the important pitfalls in team teaching which should be avoided when constructing the team and putting the plan into action.[2]

Lack of Proper Facilities

Many schools proceed into team teaching without the proper facilities. This easily would negate any advantages inherent in the program. Team teaching requires facilities which have often been considered optional in the teaching-learning situation, i.e., readily available audio-visual aids; a large auditorium with proper lighting and ventilation for at least 100 to 150 pupils, blackout drapes and the proper acoustics. This is why the worked-over cafeteria room is often inadequate in the makeshift teaching team program. Then there is the need for the well-stocked library with the special materials so necessary in modern programs which are based on

---

[1] R. H. Anderson and D. P. Mitchell, "Team Teaching, New Learning Concepts Demand Changes in School Plant Design," *The Nation's Schools*, LXV (June, 1960), 75-82. In this same article the authors discuss the efficacy of the present motto: "In Flexibility we trust." *Loc. cit.*, 76.
[2] A circular publication entitled the "Easton High School Team Teaching Program," describing the program in its entirety, is available at a cost of $1.00 from the Easton Area Joint High School System, Easton, Penna.

interdisciplinary disciplines. Often the teaching team program calls for carrels (language-arts, etc.), and adequate seminar rooms, for the small-group lessons. The key emphasis here is on flexibility, but unfortunately the traditional school building offers little of it, and "we found that converting this old machine to do a new job would be very costly," says William W. Caudill, a widely-known school architect.[3]

The Myth of Expandability

There always are schools which attempt to find and justify the "short-run" or the "stop-gap" procedure. Some of these even use the "flexible" sliding door to provide space adaptability and obtain the large-room lecture hall! Several high schools in New York City used the expandable-area sliding door idea in 1926. There is nothing new about this concept. What was learned then should not be forgotten now, and that is that this conversion is not a magical one — the noise still flows through and makes for a most disturbing small seminar area. In other words the school sacrifices the entire area for only one purpose. This is shortsighted planning, and long-range planning makes the best use of all facilities.

✓ Proper Staff Utilization

The successful programs in team teaching (*supra*) have created an "apex" or "hierarchy" of team teachers. In these programs the team leaders are compensated financially for the added responsibilities concomitant with leadership. Many schools have attempted to create team teaching on a "no-cost" basis, and have avoided both compensation and prestige for team leaders. This is a pitfall which easily can and should be avoided.[4] It is possible that when the chairman of the team receives special recognition in the way of money, title, or prestige the other members of the team are likely to resent this evidence of status and superiority. If there is to be a ladder of professionalism with its advantages, however, then teachers should respect and expect adequate compensation for added re-

---

[3]William W. Caudill, "False Economies in Schoolhouse Construction," *Saturday Review* (May 18, 1963), 72-74, and 84.

[4]For the analysis on the shortcomings of our conventional use of teachers see the two-part film report (57 minutes), "And No Bells Ring," narrated by Hugh Downs. This film can be ordered from the National Association of Secondary School Principals, 1201 Sixteenth Street, N. W., Washington 6, D. C., for $3.00.

sponsibility and leadership. Team teaching works best when teachers are free of ego involvement and professional bias.

Recruiting for the Team Project

This raises another problem. Teachers should be chosen for a team on the basis of their ability to contribute to the team; therefore in order to avoid any conflict of personalities the duties of all team members should be clearly defined. Often this is not provided for in the preliminary planning, but it should be. A team cannot have two leaders.

Interestingly enough, there have not been many problems of interpersonnel relationships in team teaching. The pitfall here is that team teaching breaks sharply with tradition, and teachers ordinarily trained for the isolated, traditional classroom come unprepared for new behavior patterns and expectations. To avoid this an inservice training program should be started prior to the inception of the team teaching project. During the training for team effectiveness it would be well to determine each member's strength. Some teachers are at their best with large groups, some with small groups, etc.

Curriculum Supervision

Another pitfall in team teaching is proper curriculum supervision. Careful guidance of teachers and curriculum supervision are the essence of any successful school venture, and team teaching is no exception. Enthusiastic teachers faced with large timeblocks often need proper curriculum assistance so that these can provide a firm core of instruction, and not dissipate instructional time. Many schools are so concerned with the structure of "the team" that they forget the main objective of the teaching team — to improve the quality of instruction. Proper curriculum direction will assure that each member of the team will carry his share of the work load and contribute to the team's objectives. A teaching team is not a refuge for inferior teaching.

Innovation Without Foundation

Many of the problems and pitfalls of team teaching seem to be directly related to one another, and sometimes result from the poor planning and poor staff utilization. This can be seen, for example, when schools do not look before they leap into team teaching. This is the "jump into prestige" and is not sound educational practice. The experiment seems to be innovation for innovation's sake. One writer warns against this by saying: "If we are to modify present patterns of teaching and expend tax dollars to do it, we must have clear objectives for our actions on which we are ready to stand the test of objective evaluation."[5]

No Safety in Numbers

When team teaching is simply identified with large group instruction, only this and nothing more, then we are fostering a situation which should be limited — that is the large lecture class with no further extension of learning. The school which does this has fallen into "the pitfall of numbers," and there is no magic of learning here primarily because the school proceeded without a blueprint for proper learning.[6]

Careful Planning for Foundation Building

The Importance of Time

Many pitfalls in team teaching can be avoided by careful planning. A great number of teachers involved find that little time was scheduled for the many meetings so necessary to team teaching. In team teaching teachers need time to organize and co-ordinate the entire program. The school administrator who tends to sell the concept to his staff on a "business as usual during altercations" basis condemns this team project to failure from the very beginning.

Proper Counseling

Team teaching often makes it difficult to meet the individual needs of all the pupils in a large group; therefore it is necessary to build into the program proper provision for sound guidance and

[5]Gregory R. Anrig, "Promising and Perplexing Aspects of Large Group Teaching Experiments," *Locus of Change: Staff Utilization Studies, The Bulletin,* NASSP, XLVI, No. 270 (January, 1962), 255.
[6]Arvel B. Clark, "An Appraisal of Team Teaching," *California Journal of Secondary Education,* XXXVI, No. 7 (November, 1961), 441-44.

counseling. Many schools overlook this because their premise is that several teachers banded into a team will produce some form of instructional magic — it won't.[7] This is a pitfall that can easily be avoided during the planning period, i.e., before the program is put into practice.

The Problem of Grouping

Another pitfall is one that should be familiar to all of us. It is a stumbling-block labelled "grouping." To expect that presentations can be made to a large-group audience (100-150 pupils) on the assumption that students in a heterogeneous assembly are equally skilled in grasping the basic instruction is unrealistic. To avoid this pitfall it is necessary during the planning and programming stage to recognize student differences and make provision for them.

Need for Public Understanding

Some educators advise that gradual change based upon gradual acceptance is the most successful way to proceed. Most of us view new ideas with some suspicion and tend to be hostile to abrupt changes which seem to have little rationale to commend or justify them. In public relations, for example, it is necessary before embarking upon team teaching that parents understand the entire program, and especially the objectives, and show a willingness to co-operate with the demands of the new program. Educators should make an effort to improve the image of the new school — avoid the "sweeping under the rug" technique — and thus share the excitement and stimulation which any new program offers. In this way the educator will stay away from the pitfall of misunderstanding.

When team teaching is being planned in your school it would be sensible to include in the project a committee of citizens for "community resources and research" as a part of the planning team.

---

[7]One definition of team teaching states: "Obviously a teaching team is a combination of persons assigned to the same group of students at the same time for instructional purposes. The rationale is that the total educational accomplishment of the team is greater than the 'sum' of the teaching attainments which the teachers would reach in regular individual situations." Robert H. Johnson and M. D. Lobb, "Transformation of the Sacred Secondary School Schedule," *California Journal of Secondary Education*, XXXV (February, 1962), 98.

After all, citizens are often asked to contribute to the school; then why should they not be invited to become a part of its team teaching program? Naturally it is expected that citizens will serve as teacher aids and as resource talent in the instructional program. If the early stages of planning the team teaching program are handled properly most parents will be enthusiastic about the program! Much of the future success of this program depends upon the initial planning and this should be done carefully, without haste or "participation panic."

Presentation Phase of Team Teaching

One of the pitfalls of team teaching stems from its instructional method of procedure. There is a great deal of emphasis on the presentation step of the learning process. This develops naturally from the drama of the large-group lecture with its almost circus-like presentation of the basic material. The presentation phase occupies the center of the learning stage and tends to overshadow the small group learning phase where the necessary individual learning may take place. An overt attempt should be made to balance the two phases and to structure the small-group phase so that it meets the needs of the student and thus becomes a very meaningful part of his team teaching experience. In other words there should be a direct relationship of learner to content when using the large-group instruction. The amount of interaction required between instructor and student should determine, to some extent, the size of the learning group, and the curriculum must be devised to suit large—and small—group instruction respectively. After all the golden goal should be improved curriculum and not team teaching as an activity for its own sake.[8]

Methods of Proper Evaluation

One of the big problems in team teaching which could become a serious pitfall since it would ultimately influence the "image" of that project is how to properly evaluate what the pupil has learned. Can we readily use traditional measuring instruments to determine

---

[8]A fine analysis on team teaching is to be found in Harold Howe II, "The Curriculum, The Team, And The School: An Examination of Relationships," *California Journal of Secondary Education*, XXXVII, No. 6 (October, 1962), 353-61.

the effectiveness of large-group experimentation? Must we devise new methods of evaluation? If evaluation and objectives go hand in hand then perhaps evaluation should be reconsidered when objectives are changed.[9]

Perhaps it will be necessary to devise tests which are more suited to what has been taught in the large-group and small-group instruction. One observer who has had extensive experience with team teaching pointed out that the range which standard tests measure is very limited and that ". . .it becomes apparent that available standard tests provide an inadequate basis for judgment in those areas and that new instruments capable of discriminating among such matters are needed."[10]

There is little doubt that the limitations of standardized tests hamper a true evaluation of team teaching and more creative approaches to evaluation are needed. Note, for example, that in four studies made in the Claremont Program (Upland High School, Upland, Calif., Chemawa Junior High School, Riverside, Calif., Fullerton and Sunny Hills High School, Fullerton, Calif., and Azusa High School, Azusa, Calif.) it was judged in each of the studies that "from these data one would conclude that the Teaching Team Program. . .did not significantly affect the areas of student achievement as measured by (type of test used)."[11] One must be aware that the standardized tests were designed to evaluate traditional programs, and perhaps were not capable of assaying new programs based upon new concepts.

Standards of Assessment

Whatever assumptions one has about team teaching, these must in time be validated by certain standards of assessment. Not all areas need to be evaluated objectively. In some subjective professional evaluation is certainly more desirable than standardized measurement. This is because many aspects, such as the effectiveness of flexible staff utilization, do not lend themselves to objective

[9]F. G. Macomber and L. Siegel, "A Study in Large-Group Teaching Procedures," *Educational Record*, XXXVIII (July, 1957), 220.
[10]Malcolm P. Douglass, "Team Teaching: Fundamental Change or Passing Fancy?" California Teachers Association *Journal*, LIX, No. 2 (March, 1963), 27.
[11]*Third Annual Report, Claremont Teaching Team Program, 1961-62*, Claremont Graduate School and University Center, Claremont, Calif.

judgements. This introduces another important innovation in the evaluation of team teaching, and that is that varied interpretative measuring instruments will have to be used in team teaching if a true analytical picture is to be obtained, and as in the traditional program the new program should be under constant evaluative scrutiny.[12]

The Problem of Scheduling

Another pitfall in planning team teaching, and certainly an area that presents great difficulty, is the scheduling phase. Scheduling the school day is difficult enough but when a school has to arrange large blocks of time for various teams and take into consideration the assignment of teachers into teams and pupils into groups the problems become monumental! Perhaps the best way a school

INSTRUMENTS OF EVALUATION
1. Basic standardized achievement tests.
2. Psychological tests of mental maturity for a representative sample of students.
3. Teacher questionnaire.*
4. Pupil questionnaire.
5. Teacher anecdotal observations of student behavior prior to team teaching and after team teaching.
6. Teacher time study (analysis of planning time, preparation, etc.).
7. School statistical comparative chart (dropouts, grades, etc.).
8. Teacher's team teaching progress chart.
9. Principal's "co-ordination" record of team teaching.
10. Analysis of reports of team leaders with corrective suggestions.
11. Parent questionnaire.*
12. Analysis of consultants on team teaching progress.
13. Report of school counselors and guidance team.
14. Analysis of reports from auxiliary members of the team.
15. Analysis of data obtained from subject area examinations (comparative).
16. Reaction analysis of school faculty on team teaching.
17. Master teacher report of staff utilization and performance.

should approach team teaching is to experiment in a limited way without attempting to overhaul the entire school organization at

---

*See Appendix A.
[12]See p. 126 for *Instruments of Evaluation*, both objective and subjective.

once. A simple formula is to combine two classes that are scheduled the same period and arrange for each teacher to handle the area of his strength. This means, of course, that the teachers involved should have the same free period to plan their combined program, and this "common planning" period concept follows through no matter how many teams a school organizes.[13]

The Flexible Schedule Plan

In flexible scheduling each school naturally will have to make specific modifications peculiar to its own situation. There is not as yet any set pattern or group of scheduling patterns, and yet large-group and small-group patterns of instruction call for inter-action and close coordination. Much depends on the factors of sub-jects and grade levels when attempting to block out team sched-ules. Each school should decide before proceeding into team teach-ing whether the grade level or the content is to be the unit of or-ganization, or whether the teams should be formed for a major subject area in several grades.[14] An inherent danger here is that many schools end up with "flexible scheduling in depth" but not team scheduling.

PROPER USE OF TIME. Flexible grouping, that is utilizing the large-group basis of organization for instruction, is only a part of the blueprint for team teaching. The blueprint includes "large time blocks for integrated instruction," "planning time for teacher pro-gram organization and meetings" and, of course, "a flexible sched-ule that is really flexible" and meets the needs of the program. A good team teaching program should be designed to provide a cer-tain amount of flexibility in the scheduling of classes to allow for varying time requirements, and as the curriculum changes the schedule should be reviewed.[15] Many schools have difficulty with scheduling, and have successfully used the computer as an aide. Schools should not neglect the advances in science and mathe-matics, and should willingly harness these advances to improve the

[13]G. T. Kowitz, "Problems in Teacher Utilization," *American School Board Journal*, CXXXVIII (February, 1959), 24.

[14]For excellent scheduling models as suggestions on a continuum see J. A. Brownell and H. A. Taylor, *op. cit.*, 152-155.

[15]Robert G. Andree, "Large Classes and Effective Teaching," *Clearing House*, XXXIII (February, 1959), 33.

school program. Actually we are limited only by our imagination and our ability to provide organizational planning.[16]

The Administrator and Team Teaching

Every superintendent who contemplates team teaching must make certain that he has leaders on his administrative team. Much of the success or failure of any team teaching enterprise depends on the energy and skill of the school administrator. Naturally, no school would be disposed to admit that their personnel is not capable or willing to experiment with a new program; however, although many administrators and teachers are competent not all are suited by temperament or training for team teaching. If an administrator, for example, is a "floor wax and light bulb" administrator who concentrates on the trivial problems and fails to center his attention on significant school problems, then the team teaching project could fail.[17] As the educational leader of the school he should foster the type of climate that will encourage his staff to experiment, and put into practice a program that will be beneficial to the students of the school. In the section titled "Suggested Guidelines for Establishing a Team Teaching Program," one school report on team teaching suggested: "An atmosphere conducive to the creative use of teaching talents must be established by the principal. Teachers must be encouraged to develop their individual talents and explore new ways of utilizing the skills of others."[18]

In a sense the principal becomes the co-ordinator of the teams, and he "must ensure an orderly, balanced, sequential program for the entire school. He must think, plan, and act as leader of an enterprise more diversified than formerly. . .It means an active role for him. . . ."[19]

---

[16]Alexander J. Stoddard, *Schools for Tomorrow: An Educator's Blueprint*, New York; The Fund for Advancement of Education, 1957.

[17]T. C. Gurney, M. Bleifeld, J. E. Reese, and A. K. Link, "What Responsibilities for the Principal in Organizing, Supervising and Evaluating Teaching Teams?" *The Bulletin*, NASSP, XLV (April, 1961), 115-20.

[18]Harvey R. Wall and R. W. Reasoner, "Team Teaching," Concord, Calif., 1962. This booklet can be obtained from the Mt. Diablo School District, and is a valuable description of the results of one team teaching project.

[19]John A. Brownell and H. A. Taylor, *op. cit.*, 154.

The Principal's Role and Team Teaching

The role of the principal of a teaching team school does not as yet fit into a standard mold. It is clear, however, that at present it is the principal's responsibility to assess the recommendations of the teams, modify them, reject them, or approve them. If necessary he should involve consultant help and district office supervisory personnel in reaching decisions necessary for team teaching development. The principal should execute a keen sense of timing during this entire procedure and find ways to best coordinate team teaching changes in his school.

Preparation of Students for the Team

One of the most surprising omissions of the literature on team teaching concerns the preparation of students for team teaching.[20] After a study of hundreds of team teaching projects it can be concluded that many schools, following a policy of "unsalutary neglect," failed to prepare the most important segment of team teaching for team teaching — the student! This is a pitfall that can easily be avoided. The students should be well-oriented to the procedures to be followed, and especially briefed on the entire program, including the objectives. The orientation phase for the student ought to proceed slowly and should be a part of the incipient planning for team teaching — it will pay huge dividends later.

Avoid Pitfalls by Careful Planning

The best way to avoid pitfalls in team teaching is to foresee them, plan and guard against them. The planners of any team teaching project should be armed with a series of questions. These questions are more important than facile answers which do not improve team teaching or lull the team participants into a false sense of educational accomplishment. These questions are drawn in part, from the extensive national survey conducted by the author. Some of these questions are directly aimed at the planners of future

---

[20]See Judson T. Shaplin, "Team Teaching," *Saturday Review*, XLIV (May 20, 1961), 54-55, 70. This is a discussion of the pitfalls in team teaching and the elements common to many team teaching projects.

team teaching projects. If you are planning to use team teaching, ask yourself:

Have we any special reason for going into team teaching?

Have we allowed plenty of time for careful organizing and planning of the basic structure for team teaching?

Are the teams adequately housed in existing plant facilities?

Do the team leaders chosen have the leadership qualities so necessary to successful team teaching?

Does your flexible scheduling provide for common preparatory periods for team teachers, aides, and other teachers in the department? Is there a provision for daily and weekly planning sessions?

Is the reporting system (grading) properly tied to the objectives of team teaching?

Does your planning lend itself to continuous change and correction of abuses which appear from time to time?

Are the pupils properly grouped, and is there provision in your team teaching plan for transferring students between groups when cases warrant?

Does your plan provide for an adequate testing program to ascertain pupil progress and a method to evaluate continously the progress of the program?

Is there a balance between the large-group activity and the small-group activity, and is there opportunity for all children to be involved in the small-group program?

Has any effort been made for pre-service preparation for team teaching emphasizing the "team" aspects?

Does the plan include a use of staff analysis which utilizes the strengths of each team member and fixes the responsibilities, with equity, for each individual?

Has the program been planned in such a way that provision for student independent study is built into the schedule?

Has the curriculum been especially written for team teaching, and are the proper instructional materials available?

These are only a few of the questions the planners of prospective team teaching should ask themselves. Schools have no justification for jumping into it when they do not know how to use the techniques which make team teaching successful. The community has too great a stake in education to be contented with half measures or with education conceived in purely selfish terms. There is no magic charm to team teaching. As one group of authors warned: "Let it not be assumed that numbers guarantee success. As E. I.

Thorndike so aptly expressed it — 'Pooling the ignorance of a thousand is no more enlightening than the ignorance of one.' "[21]

The Road Toward Improved Learning

When team teaching is used properly the school is on the road toward improved learning, and it has taken the first step toward smashing the traditional mold of education which prevents change and hampers creative teaching. Team teaching, however, is not a top that is wound up and then left to spin on its own equilibrium. It is a program that needs continuous surveillance and correction and improvement. It has its pros and cons, and the participants should be aware of the advantages to be gained and the possible disadvantages that are implied in any team teaching program.

Summary

The accent today is upon change, but change brings uncertainty and many educators must learn to live with both the challenges and the uncertain future. It seems rational and logical that the answers are not to be found by jumping on any bandwagon or adopting any educational fad that happens to be in vogue at the time.

There are many fundamental questions which remain unanswered in team teaching, and there are many pitfalls in team teaching. Many times schools rush into a team teaching program without critically surveying their facilities, reviewing the staff potential, or overhauling their curriculum, and plan badly or even not at all.

Team teaching often calls for a new educational philosophy, a new blueprint for proper learning. New procedures for grouping students, new counseling methods, flexible schedules which part from the old time patterns, and the proper harnessing of community resources to learning all call for a potent public relations campaign. There are many pitfalls in team teaching (presentation methods, proper evaluation techniques, grouping and facilities problems, etc.), but these difficulties are not indigenous to team teach-

---

[21]T. M. Weiss and M. S. Morris, "Critique of the Team Approach," *Educational Forum*, XXIV (January, 1960), 207-08. Material used by permission of Kappa Delta Pi, honor society in education, copyright owners.

ing but are a part and parcel of the problems of education. The solution to many of these problems lies in careful planning.

Topics for Discussion and Study

1. Discuss the reasons why some educators fear change, while others view it as a challenge to promote better learning.
2. Do you consider the pitfalls in team teaching to be an integral part of the team teaching enterprise?
3. Why are some of the makeshift architectural facilities used in hasty team teaching projects detrimental?
4. How would you go about correcting these architectural disadvantages?
5. Make a list of those personality characteristics you would consider necessary each member of the team possess in order that the team functions properly.
6. How would you correlate team teaching with the school curriculum?
7. What are some of the problems that team teaching presents in regard to large and small grouping?
8. List the major individual needs of an elementary pupil, and explain whether a team teaching project meets or does not meet these needs.
9. Plan a public relations program which would help to "sell" team teaching in your community.
10. Team teaching calls for new methods of measurement and evaluation. Explain how you would devise new instruments of measurement.
11. Why is it necessary when planning team teaching to reconsider the scheduling of students?
12. What is the principal or administrator's rôle in planning and fostering team teaching?
13. What do you think would be the best way to prepare students for a team teaching program?
14. How would you go about setting the stage for the planning phase of team teaching?

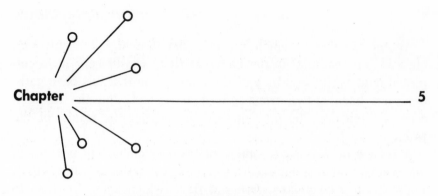

Chapter _____ **5**

AN APPRAISAL OF TEAM TEACHING: THE
PRO AND CON

An honest appraisal of team teaching is very difficult to make at this time. It is too premature. One of the reasons for this is because the experiment, in general, is still in its infancy. Harris A. Taylor states: "Definitely a maturation process must take place before a program can be considered to have reached a point where evaluation is profitable."[1]

Another reason is the fact that we have permitted ourselves to indulge in the romance that we are now revolutionaries in education when in fact American education is really the product of long tradition and evolution. The mischief of our rationalist illusion is that it leads to erroneous inferences about team teaching which is in reality based on the functions of organization and touches on the theories of learning only indirectly. It therefore becomes necessary to review the pro and con of team teaching to visualize vividly how this organizational method of instruction influences and applies to sound learning. As S. D. Thomson wisely pointed out: "Lowering the bars of rigidity does not automatically cause innovators to step forth; in fact leprechauns might."[2]

---

[1]See H. F. Olds, "Survey of a Meeting on Team Teaching (minutes)," *Committee on Team Teaching*, Chicago, 1960, 2; and D. R. Wynn and R. W. DeRemer, "Staff Utilization, Development, and Evaluation," *Review of Educational Research*, XXXI (October, 1961), 393-400.

[2]Scott D. Thomson, "Can Team Teaching Aid Learning?" *Journal of Secondary Education*, XXXVI, No. 7 (November, 1961), 424. This is an excellent article on team teaching, and sheds light on the relationship between team teaching and the learning process. See also R. O. Hahn, Jack Nelson, and Gertrude Robinson, "Team Teaching: A Second Look," *Journal of Teacher Education* (NEA), XII (December, 1961), 508-10.

Another difficulty which prevents the drawing of useful conclusions on "teaming" is the fact that there is still very little empirical data available. Much of the information that has been gathered has been drawn from subjective reports, and the research reports often describe only one phase and not the results of the program "in toto."

A review of the disadvantages of team teaching will not in any way prove that this approach to learning is ineffective, but will in many instances point to structural flaws which act as barriers to sound learning. It may be that one of the variables in team teaching has been improperly utilized, thus throwing the project out of balance. Perhaps when our assessment of team teaching is concluded we may be forced to agree with H. D. Drummond that: "The educational spotlight should be focused on the learning process, rather than on teaching."[3]

Could it be possible that many critics see team teaching as primarily a teaching instrument which denies the possibility of interaction between the teacher and student? Regardless of the present image of team teaching on the American educational scene the questioning and weighing of all the evidence available should continue. Only in this way will it be possible to determine if team teaching promises much in theory and produces little in performance. Only in this way will we be able to answer the question: Is team teaching form without substance?

The Critical Examination of Team Teaching

We know that as team teaching is used today it still is not the perfect instrument for learning; it needs to be sharpened and refined. This cannot be done by any kind of blanket condemnation but by carefully examining the variables involved in the total picture of team teaching.

In addition to philosophical and psychological implications, team teaching seems to have its dark side. In an extensive survey on team

---

[3]"An Assessment of Team Teaching," *The Shape of Education for 1962-63*, National School Public Relations Association (NEA), 1962, 25.

[4]Anne Hoppach, "Team Teaching: Form Without Substance?" National Education Association *Journal*, L (April, 1961), 47-8. In this same article the author writes: "Rather than giving aid and comfort to the 'status quo' in teaching experimentation should develop new and improved ways to put into practice the knowledge about human growth and learning which is now available. . . Team teaching is too much 'tell and test' teaching." *Ibid.*, 47.

teaching the author found the same recurring themes presented as disadvantages of team teaching.[5] These themes were:

1. Personnel selection is difficult, and there are no criteria to serve as a standard.
2. Coordination within the team could have been improved if leadership responsibilities had been designated.
3. Lecturing was overdone in the program.
4. Team teaching calls for facilities which are not available in the present school plan.
5. Independent study was not properly exploited.
6. Most of the learning became dependent on the "lecture-listen" instruction.
7. The personnel problems became overwhelming and the scheduling became too complicated.
8. Friction developed among team members due to lack of time to plan properly.
9. Team teaching with its so-called "flexible scheduling" builds rigidity into the master program.
10. Students have less freedom of choice with both teachers and courses.
11. If the team continues longer than one school year, dropouts cannot be easily replaced to maintain the team.
12. There is a lack of appropriate measuring devices and lack of clear-cut educational objectives particularly in the affective domain (interests, attitudes, values, appreciations).
13. Some students dislike being in large classes, and many do not want to accept, and often do not, the increased responsibility which is placed on the pupil in large team teaching classes.
14. Students tend to be less attentive in large lecture classes.
15. Limited curriculum materials; we have had to make our own the "slow, hard way."
16. We feel that team teaching does not meet the emotional needs of many of our pupils.
17. We found a lack of flexibility due to the pressure to conform to group testing.
18. It took the instructor a longer period of time to get to know his students, and many instructors performed on a "large-group"

---

[5]See Robert D. Ohm, "Toward a Rationale for Team Teaching," *Administrator's Notebook*, IX, No. 7 (March, 1961). In regard to the pros and cons of team teaching one author writes: "The full picture of team teaching remains to be critically tested . . . and team teaching may provide one of our most useful organizational approaches." Wally Walker, "Team Teaching: Pros and Cons," California Teacher Association *Journal*, LVIII, No. 4 (April, 1962), 17.

basis overlooking individual needs. Teaching was done en masse.

19. We found the added cost of extra equipment to be a budget problem.
20. Team teaching is too formal and learning is not as spontaneous as it should be.

These statements of the disadvantages of team teaching by various educators have some validity; however, some of this difficulty could have been avoided by more careful planning and some of the other disadvantages are open to question.[6] There is implied in this, however, that our preoccupation with educational logistics does tend to obscure the basic principles of learning, and that reshuffling the tools of learning will somehow produce some strange magic.

A Practical Look at Team Teaching

Many educators have taken a long, hard, practical look at team teaching.[7] In general they complain about the large-group phase of team teaching. Many argue that this lecture method places an added burden on the teachers because it calls for a great deal of preparation; that it discourages student participation; that reluctant learners hide in the crowd; and that the heavy burden of recording attendance and mass student manipulation is time-consuming. Some educators have claimed that large-group instruction calls for a very special approach towards learning which is foreign to many teachers, and that because of different work patterns and educational philosophies teachers find it difficult to work on a team and thus often compete with each other. This is detrimental to the team approach. Perhaps this is one of the negative aspects of the plan, but then it is possible to educate teachers to work as a team, i.e., to become imbued with the "group liability" idea.[8]

---

[6] See W. B. Mitchell, "Why Try Team Teaching?" NASSP *Bulletin*, XLVI (January, 1962), 247-52, and S. R. Johnson, "Team Teaching? Enthusiasm is High," New York State Educational *Bulletin*, L (November, 1962), 14-16. A very useful discussion on team teaching is Robert L. Shayon, radio program on team teaching in the "Everybody's Mountain" Series of the National Association of Education Broadcasters, 14 Gregory Hall, Urbana, Illinois. This tape is available on a rental basis.

[7] See D. Baynham, "School of the Future in Operation," *Phi Delta Kappan*, XLII (May, 1961), 350-54; and Robert N. Bush, "Searching Appraisal of New Developments," *Journal of Secondary Education*, XXXVII (October, 1962), 321-6.

[8] J. S. Butterweck, "Teachers on a Team," *Pennsylvania School Journal*, LVI (October, 1957), p. 57, and Francis S. Chase, "The Schools I Hope to See," National Education Association *Journal*, XLVI (March, 1957), 164-166.

Leadership on the Team

Some educators try to create teams without leaders, assuming that group dynamics will provide the necessary leadership — and are surprised when their team runs aground due to the lack of an educational rudder! Teaming needs strong leadership, and one of the difficulties which borders on the area of disadvantages is the fact that few teachers are properly trained for this type of leadership.[9] A leader of a team of teachers must have a broad background, be open to new ideas, and be able to coordinate and surprise the team teaching plan. He must be above all a master teacher himself since the team teachers look to him for direction and example. If he attains the position of team leader as a reward for "galloping conformity" to administrative edicts and is not a master teacher, then the team has an organizational climate that dooms it to failure.[10]

Critics of the Team Concept

Others critics of team teaching say that one of the disadvantages of team teaching today in many of our schools is that most teams have been arranged around existing time schedules, consequently many team members teach as many if not more hours than before. This situation leaves little time for proper planning, burdens the teachers, and finally brings about diminishing educational returns which cast a dark shadow over the team teaching program. In this situation, the school is trying to buy team teaching at bargain prices — and it cannot be done!

Independent Study

Educators seem to be fond of the argument that team teaching does not meet the individual needs of the students. This is, however, not a valid disadvantage, nor should it be considered as such since the independent, individual study opportunities built into the team teaching program can provide for any heterogeneous student body. There is little doubt that successful independent

---

[9]E. M. Cobett, "Different Approach to Team Teaching," *Ohio Schools,* XXXVIII (November, 1960), 10-11, and H. D. Drummond, "Team Teaching: An Assessment," *Educational Leadership,* XIX (December, 1961), 160-6, also the *Education Digest,* XXVII (February, 1962), 5-8.

[10]J. P. Dix, "Team Teaching Requires Team Spirit," *School and Community,* XLIX (November, 1962), 27.

study is tied directly to emotional and mental maturation; however, it is a part of the team teaching program to develop self-responsibility for only in this way can each pupil obtain the maximum benefits from a team situation.[11]

The Price of Team Teaching

Some qualified observers believe that team teaching is more costly and this is a budgetary factor which has to be considered.[12] In the main, however, the big question is: Has team teaching proved effective? It is in answering this question that many critics seek to define the advantages and disadvantages of team teaching.

The Effectiveness of Team Teaching

In almost all the literature and research on team teaching the same theme appears. It is a theme which is certainly open to question, and reveals the vulnerability of team teaching. In studying the summary and conclusions of hundreds of team teaching projects one is amazed to find that the schools candidly admit that "the limited instruments of measurements have made it impossible to show superior achievement. It has been shown that children achieve as well academically as in the self-contained classroom."[13]

Data on a Team Teaching Program

Although both objective and subjective techniques were used to evaluate the Jefferson Counyt R-1 High School program in Jefferson County, Colorado, the conclusion reached was that pupils in the experimental classes did just as well as those in the

---

[11]"The psychologists are not very happy about team teaching in elementary schools because they feel that young children need the security of a single teacher and a single class group." J. J. B. Dempster, "America Explores Team Teaching," Times Educational Supplement, 2449 (April 27, 1962), 826. This is a part of a series on team teaching by British writers, see Numbers 2450, 2451, 2453, 2454, and 2455.

[12]Robert H. Anderson, "Team Teaching in the Elementary School," The Education Digest, XXV (November, 1959), 26-28.

[13]"The Norwalk Plan of Team Teaching," Third Report, 1960-61, Norwalk Board of Education, Norwalk, Conn., 7. "Data reported to date show that team teaching results are no less satisfactory than those from typical conventional teaching in elementary and secondary schools." Robert H. Anderson, "Team Teaching," NEA Journal, I., No. 3 (March, 1961), 54.

regular classes.[14] This conclusion is not calculated to produce great enthusiasm for team teaching. The most that can be said about the program is that it was not a failure and showed some indication of a slight amount of success.

Exploring the Possibilities

In his findings on another team teaching project one writer concluded: "We strongly believe there is much merit in this newer concept of teaching secondary students, and we hope to explore the possibilities to the limit of our ingenuity, physical facilities, and teaching skills. We certainly hope to have more tangible results on the validity of this belief we hold."[15] The conclusion that achievement under team teaching is "as good as" that in control groups leaves much to be desired, and places the disadvantage of adequate evaluation in a new light.

Lack of Objective Evidence

Most of the reports which have attempted to evaluate the recent experiments in team teaching indicate that there currently is little concrete evidence that improved learning results from team teaching. Much of the enthusiasm for the program seems to stem from subjective elements which do not lend themselves to objective measurements (*supra*).[16] One critical observer asks a most pertinent question: "Should not the creation of problems so costly in human resources and perhaps in money be offest by quite superior learning outcomes?"[17] The answer, of course, should be a loud, thunderous "yes." Theoretically, team teaching should be a

[14]Robert H. Johnson, M. D. Lobb, and L. G. Swenson, "An Extensive Study of Team Teaching and Schedule Modification in the Jeffereson County, Colorado School District R-1," The NASSP *Bulletin*, XLIV (January, 1960), 79-93.

[15]H. A. Clawson, "English and Science Studies in Mattoon Senior High School," NASSP *Bulletin*, LIV (January, 1960), 257-263, and see M. S. Norton, "Approaches to Team Teaching," NASSP *Bulletin*, XLIV (October, 1960), 89-92, and C. E. Gross, "Team Teaching in Pittsburgh," *Education Digest*, XXVIII (November, 1962), 12-15.

[16]Note that the questionnaire is widely used in obtaining data on team teaching. In the Claremont questionnaire it was reported that: "Students' resistance to teams definitely increased in their second and third year on teams." *Second Annual Report to the Ford Foundation By the Claremont Teaching Team Program 1960-61*, Claremont Graduate School and University Center, Claremont, Cal., 45.

[17]Anne Hoppach, "Team Teaching: Form Without Substance?" National Education *Journal*, L (April, 1961), 48.

step forward in providing learning opportunities. The traditional concepts of rigidity in class size, curriculum and scheduling are destroyed. This in itself should provide many advantages that would facilitate learning.

There is little double that the shadow cast over team teaching is due in part to the fact that many of the team projects are inadequately reported, probably because our present research pattern is much too broad. We need to concentrate on specific questions, isolate the many variables of team teaching, and weigh our evidence more carefully so that the results of team projects can be more conclusive; then and only then, will we be able to see team teaching in its true light.

The Realities of Team Teaching

To see team teaching in its true light educators should try to interpret the present evidence on team teaching projects in the cold light of neutrality. The results of these projects should be described with words not couched in some kind of "establishment philosophy," which presumes the validity of a cluster of unfounded value judgements. This is the point that G. E. Mueller makes when he writes: "The educator wants to enable the pupil to lead a better life than would be possible without his direction, and the pupil trusts, more or less, that the educator is privy to the secret of this better life. This mutual faith is not altered by the most opposed concepts of what is believed to be 'better.' "[18]

In a sense team teaching is not just an amendment to traditional practice but involves a fundamental departure from it. This type of approach to learning presumes that the school will move from a procedural method of staff distribution out into the entire field of curriculum and learning. In time perhaps sound team teaching practices will allay "the current anxiety that there has been a serious letdown in standards of instruction as a result of modern educational procedures."[19]

---

[18]Gustave E. Mueller, *Education Limited* (Norman, Okla.: University of Oklahoma Press, 1949), 13. See, for an excellent anlysis of the conflicting concepts of education, Richard D. Mosier, *The American Temper, Patterns of Our Intellectual Heritage*, Berkeley, Calif.: University of California Press, 1952), 290-94.

[19]John S. Brubacher, "The Challenge to Philosophize about Education," Nelson B. Henry, ed., *Modern Philosophies and Education*, Fifty-Fourth *Yearbook* of the National Society for the Study of Education (Chicago: University of Chicago Press, 1955), 15.

In his poetic essay "Of the Knowledge and Characters of Men," Alexander Pope speaks about being "right by chance."[20] If education is really a dialectical process of great importance than the element of chance must be reduced to a minimum. We realize, however, that certainty in the affairs of education, no matter how desirable, is rarely possible. The best evidence of the results of team teaching projects is obtained from comprehensive and professional observation, free of bias and self-interest. It is possible to give only a few general words of advice. The chief of these must always be the old maxim, "Be skeptical — regard every facile claim with doubt."

Myths Surrounding Team Teaching

The Place of the Aide

On the debit side of the team teaching ledger there are several facile claims that need microscopic examination. These are what we call myths — unreal concepts that give educational ideas a charismatic aurora of certain success. Let us examine, for example, the concept of the aide (*supra*) in team teaching. There is no doubt that the use of auxiliary personnel for all nonteaching tasks would be most welcome in teaching regardless of which instructional plan was in use.[21] There remains, however, the expense involved in using aides, the difficulty of obtaining qualified personnel, and the problem of efficiently working the aide into the instructional program. Most educators are so enamored with the idea of teaching aides that they tend to overlook the concommitant problems which often accompany their use. Not only are aides costly, although it may be argued that they are well worth the expense, but many of them are not professionally trained to work with young people, and in many areas of the nation their use is often vitiated by legal limitations.[22] It is suggested by some careless advocates that aides be used for supervisory work, and this is fine, but unfortunately they get carried away and go beyond

---

[20]Douglas Grant, ed., *Poems of Alexander Pope* (London: Penguin Books, Ltd., 1950), 130.
[21]David T. Turney, "The Instructional Secretary as Used by Classroom Teachers," *Peabody Research and Development Program*, Nashville, Tennessee, 1959.
[22]See for example *The State of California Education Code*, State of California, Dept. of Education, Vol. I (Sacramento, Calif.: California Printing Office, 1961), 517.

this and argue that aides be used in remedial group instruction. Here we have a dangerous assumption. Remedial group instruction belongs rightfully to an expert — one trained in this area. This is what Curt Stafford calls "activities incongruous with professional training."[23] Yes, we have a large pool of educated men and women who can help to lighten the load and ease the educational burden; however, it is both foolish and unprofessional to permit the aide to rush into important professional areas without proper preparation. If we agree that teachers need to be both well-educated and well-prepared to do a professional job then we cannot turn over these complex areas of learning to amateurs.

Teacher Recruitment

Many educators argue that the use of the teaching aide is a sound basis for teacher recruitment. This is a questionable premise. Teaching is a lifelong art, and the best that can be said is that the teaching aide may be introduced into the mysterious world of teaching and thus may be able to take the first step on the long road toward successful teaching.

Realities of Team Teaching in Action

Problems in the Field

Team teaching programs as described by the current literature are often filled with paeans of joy about the so-called new-found method of instruction, but the sharp critic can find weaknesses. Throughout the descriptive literature and observation in the field *in situ,* one finds inflexibility, problems of pace and planning and the need for improved methods of communication.[24] In some team teaching programs there has been difficulty with scheduling, a heavy administrative burden, difficulties with proper counseling, the inability to motivate because of exceptionally large groups, problems with school interruptions which broke into the time-block, and the difficulty of obtaining course outlines to fit the

---

[23]Curt Stafford, "Teacher Time Utilization with Teacher Aides," *The Journal of Educational Research,* LVI, No. 2 (October, 1962), 81.
[24]See J. S. Bowes, "A Venture in Team Teaching," *The Social Studies,* LIV, No. 7 (December, 1963), 257-59.

team teaching program. Obviously some of these problems are common to everyday school life, but many of them were aggravated and not relieved by team teaching programs. In part, some of the semantic difficulty in regard to team teaching is caused by the dialogue, not necessarily the controversy, that goes on about team teaching. Many are not quite sure what team teaching is and consequently argue from different premises. People who engage in these arguments are like the two washerwomen Sydney Smith observed leaning out of their back windows and quarreling with each other across the alley: "They could never agree," Smith said, "because they were arguing from different premises." Perhaps W. E. Arnold is correct in saying that "the term itself has no specific meaning and is used as a name for many wrong things."[25]

Results of One Project

We know that there is no fixed formula for team teaching, but surely one would expect much more than the innocuous conclusion reached by Taffel in his team teaching experiment. In this novel team method of teaching a first course in high school physics the investigator reported no significant differences in achievement between the experimental and the control groups. On the questionnaire on team teaching, however, students and teachers responded favorably, and the conclusion reached here was that team teaching was a "practical alternative for teaching academically gifted students."[26] In view of all the praise that has been showered upon team teaching this seems to be a rather cryptic result, and surprisingly when educators really come to grips with the results of team teaching they are many times embarrassed by the lack of concrete, verifiable evidence. "Oh, but the students like it!" say some of the educators. I submit to you that the students also like some forms of music which are sheer madness! This is a poor criterion. Perhaps another problem which we have not faced squarely in this developmental period is that most of us may be unaware that "where team teaching is supported, there is an

[25]W. E. Arnold, "Is Team Teaching the Answer?" *School and Society*, XCI (December 14, 1963), 407-09.

[26]R. A. Gibboney et al, "Team Teaching," *Review of Educational Research*, XXXIII, No. 3 (June, 1963), 288-89.

evident gap between the acceptance of the idea and its implementation."[27]

The Student Faces Team Teaching

This raises a host of questions which have not as yet been answered by the enthusiasts of team teaching. What happens to me as a student when I am reduced to a lecture note-taker? Since we are now going to have all kinds of specialists in the team teaching program, which of the specialists do I see when I have a problem with my term paper? What happens to me if I am a potential dropout? Could it be true that "Dr. Trump's plan has inspired a summary steeped in deception and cynical in meaning"?[28] Could it be true that team teaching throws a shadow over the individual pupil? Do the teachers see team teaching as an opportunity for leadership or as an operational method which suppresses individuality? Only time may supply definite answers to these questions, but it is necessary to raise the right questions if we are to build upon the present foundations.

The Magnetism of Team Teaching

Team teaching has been very well received in many schools. It is an educational magnet which has attracted teachers by offering a new alternative to the present emergency, which old conventional methods could not do. Team teaching seems to be a clarion call for action — a dramatic approach to learning and teaching. Here again the flamboyance of team teaching obscures the possibility that it contains the seeds of its own distortion. Team teaching presents certain challenges to the teaching profession. Are teachers willing to work as a team? Would team teaching add to the "committee" load which teachers already abhor? Is team teaching really the road to improved professional teaching conditions?

Economics of Team Teaching

Very little has been said about the economics of team teaching. We know that many foundations have gallantly supported it, but

---

[27]"Administrator's Guide to Team Teaching," *Education Digest*, XXIX (September, 1963, 33.
[28]Laurence Niblett, "No Bells Ring for Dr. Trump," *The Bulletin* of the National Association of Secondary-School Principals, XLVI, No. 272 (March, 1962), 91.

because of the many variables it is very difficult to measure its basic costs.[29]. Statements like "$5,000 per year for each of three typical teams in an elementary school; $1,500 per year for each typical team in a high school" are not definitive guidelines.[30] A great deal depends upon the type of teams organized, the locale, and the type of curriculum which is structured into the team teaching project.

Emphasis on Independent Study

On the credit side of the educational ledger team teaching offers the high hope of great expectations for a new horizon. Many educators predict that in a few years many schools will be experimenting with various forms of team teaching. This appears to be the present trend. There are many reasons for this. The schools have often been accused of perpetuating adolescence and the burden of the indictment is that the schools do not challenge the student. Perhaps in underexpecting we misuse what Robert Merton called the self-fulfilling prophecy: the tendency for people to respond as others expect them to. Team teaching, with its emphasis upon independent study, attempts to elicit mature response from the student and develop a feeling of growth and maturity. When we treat pupils as irresponsible children, as we have often done in the past, we not only obtain childish responses (the self-fulfilling prophecy) and disenchant the good student but also mislead the less able student in creating false standards and a false sense of competence.

Improved Teacher Relationships

In many projects on team teaching throughout the country the recurrent theme of commendation has been that team teaching helps to improve teacher relationships. Teachers are brought into closer contact and learn to work together when involved in team teaching. This tends to break down the walls of isolationism and

---

[29]An excellent assay of this is Robert A. Watson, "People Not Projects Will Improve Education," *American School Board Journal*, CXLVII, No. 5 (November, 1963), 9-12.

[30]Andrew Hamilton, "Team Teaching: How Good Is It?" *Reader's Digest* (May, 1964), 169-172. Reprinted with permission from the May, 1964, *Reader's Digest.* Copyright 1964 by The Reader's Digest Association, Inc. Condensed from the *PTA Magazine.*

it is a short jump from team teaching to group co-ordination. This
is not to say that liability for the educational process is vitiated
among members. It is rather to say if we accept the basic concept
that education is a team enterprise then we have no alternative
but to improve personnel relationships and keep the channels of
communication open.

Some of the cynics in education have charged recently that the
involvement of teachers in curriculum change is largely mythical,
with most of the administrators arbitrarily installing an innovation
and then preparing teachers to handle it. It is difficult to determine the veracity of such generalizations, and an administrator
would be indeed shortsighted to proceed in such a medieval manner. Teachers have found that team teaching really offers an opportunity to take part in the constant planning and revision of
the curriculum, and that many times administrators encourage
them to be creative in this area. In this respect team teaching encourages teachers toward a more professional outlook and makes
them real partners in the educational enterprise, not clerks or
rubber stamps.

A NEW MEDIA FOR LEARNING. Through the medium of team teaching teachers are learning and acquiring a new respect for the
diverse areas of knowledge. In the past both pupils and teachers
were restricted by curriculum limits; the teacher restrained by the
limits of the subject and the pupil's horizon narrowed by the limits
of the grade level expectations. Team teaching enables students
to become genuinely involved in sound enrichment programs and
solves the problem presented by pupils who exceed grade level expectations.[31] The teachers involved gained new insights into the
relatedness of various subject areas and discovered that the
strengths and talents of the members of the team could be used
to support the team teaching plan.

Improving the Quality of Teaching

Experience has shown that team teaching has provided a better
correlation of subject matter; improved the curriculum; improved

[31]"The Gifted Student: Research Projects Concerning Elementary and Sec-
ondary Students," OE-35016, Co-operative Research Monograph No. 2, U. S.
Dept. of Health, Education, and Welfare (Washington, D. C.: Government
Printing Office, 1963), 1-19.

the quality of teaching in many areas via the use of aides (relieved the teacher of many housekeeping chores); made more efficient use of space and school equipment; stimulated practices that depart from traditional organization (elimination of grade lines, etc.); and in short has given a fill-up to a wide range of other school improvement programs.[32]

We should watch the results of team teaching projects with high hope and not hopeful wishes. The many challenges in education often bring about a sense of urgency to make changes faster than is necessary or desirable. Team teaching no doubt will go through many phases of development, and its success in part will depend upon the improvements made in education in general because it is an integral part of educational change.[33]

Summary

Any attempt to evaluate the many team teaching projects at this time would be premature. This is not to say that it would not be unprofitable in some way, for we learn by experimentation and taking stock is an integral part of educational improvement program. Unfortunately, much of the information on team teaching must be examined critically because it contains many variables. We need to continue experimentation in numerous areas of education before we can thoroughly understand those problems which belong primarily to education in general and are the result of a team teaching project.

One thing is certain, however; careful planning will help preclude the many pitfalls in team teaching. Teachers will in the future prepare themselves to work on a team, to become more proficient in team leadership as they grow professionally, and to become skilled in handling large blocks of time.

The realities of team teaching are such that they cannot be ignored. The semantics surrounding it will have to be clarified,

---

[32]For a representative list of schools active in team teaching programs see David W. Beggs III, ed., *Team Teaching: Bold New Venture* (Indianapolis, Ind.: Unified College Press, Inc., 1964), App. II., 188.

[33]For the background on team teaching see "The Antecedents of Team Teaching," *School and Society*, XCI (December 1, 1963), 393-407. Also Medill Blair and Richard G. Woodward, *Team Teaching in Action* (Boston: Houghton Mifflin Co., 1964).

and this, in part, may come about when a large bulk of the experiments in this area have helped educators to crystallize their thinking on team teaching.

Topics for Discussion and Study

1. Why is it so difficult to make an objective appraisal of team teaching at this time?

2. Make a list of those "variables in team teaching" which might throw the project out of balance.

3. Do you think that team teaching is merely a "teaching instrument" or a method of instructional procedure?

4. What would you consider the most serious disadvantage which might result from team teaching?

5. Does the large-group method of presentation offer advantages or disadvantages in learning?

6. Describe how you would prepare interne-teachers for team teaching or some form of it.

7. Could it be possible that team teaching meets the individual needs of a student in a much better way than the old traditional approach?

8. Make a tentative list of the vital and necessary costs to be included in a budget for a teaching team of four teachers, an aide, an interne-teacher, plus a counselor and a master teacher for a school science-English team.

9. What would you consider some of the most serious limitations of team teaching?

10. Inflexibility, problems of pace and planning, and the need for better methods of communication present difficulties for the team. How would you plan a team so these could be controlled?

11. Make a list of the host of new questions which a team teaching project raises. How would you attempt to answer these questions?

12. Do you feel that all teachers could profit from serving on a team? Does the team really create a "group" feeling among teachers? Will a team project draw the teachers and the administrator into a "feeling of common enterprise" which could help to improve the curriculum?

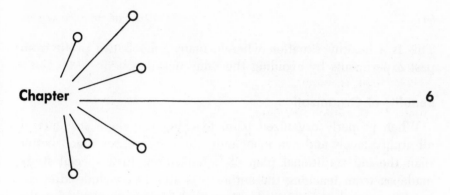

Chapter _____ **6**

THE ADVANTAGES OF TEAM TEACHING FOR THE
FUTURE SCHOOL

The effort to discredit team teaching by distortion is doomed to failure. Faced with serious questioning as to its motives and capacities, team teaching has much to offer other than optimism. One of the difficulties one has to face when making a survey of different approaches to learning is that of threading out shortcomings which properly belong to the project, i.e., those resulting from the project itself and directly related to the project. Many times problems are laid at the doorstep of team teaching which are an intrinsic part of the entire educational pattern; they exist outside of the realm of team teaching and should be attacked directly. An excellent example of this is the problem of time loss due to excessive extracurricular school activities. Such a time loss and team teaching are not directly related but are instead a matter of preserving the time blocks, keeping them closed so that team teaching scheduling can be effective. The realities of team teaching at this early developmental stage should not in any way detract from its great possibilities and inherent advantages.

It is not to be expected that all educators acquire a "Utopian mentality" toward team teaching. On the contrary, it is advisable to be most critical; however, the fact that team teaching was unsuccessful in some schools does not negate its many advantages.[1]

---

[1]On the concept of a "Utopian mentality" see Karl Mannheim, *Ideology and Utopia* (New York, 1936), 192-263.

This is a healthy situation wherein many schools can profit from past experiments by avoiding the same mistakes.

Benefits of Organization

When properly organized team teaching can serve students of all ability levels and can meet individual differences much better than the old traditional plan of organization. In a special study made on team teaching the author was able to conclude after extensive research that "An advantage that is often overlooked is the greater satisfaction the teachers received because of the team situation. Teachers were thus able to see the fruition of their labor. . .The end result was that the teacher did a much better and more effective job, and the students tended to be better adjusted and to receive a better education."[2]

Most educators are convinced that team teaching aids learning, and that it is the highway of the future.[3] In its analysis of their plan the Norwalk District concluded: "The Norwalk Plan has been a catalytic agent for improved instruction in the entire school system. It has stimulated use of newer audio-visual devices and instructional material. It has fostered a more concerted effort on curriculum revision, improved instructional techniques, more flexible grouping practices and more cooperative effort on the part of teachers not directly participating in team teaching. In short, the plan has had many positive effects both within and without the program."[4]

Pros and Cons

Other educators say that from their experience with team teaching they have found that their learning situation is improved because of the stimulation brought about by the comprehensive use

---

[2]Robert J. Loney, "A Presentation of the Students' Reports of the Kinds of Help Received from the Upland High School Teaching Team," M. A. thesis, Claremont Graduate School and University Center, 1961, 71-72, and Frank C. Mayer and James H. Woolridge, "Preparing for Team Teaching at West Clermont," *American School Board Journal*, CXLV (July, 1961), 10.

[3]Lloyd S. Michael, "Team Teaching," *The Bulletin* of the National Association of Secondary-School Principals, XLVII, No. 283 (May, 1963), 36-63.

[4]See "The Norwalk Plan of Team Teaching," *Third Report*, 1960-1961, Norwalk Board of Education, Norwalk, Conn., 7; and John R. Ginther and William A. Shroyer, "Team Teaching in English and History at the 11th Grade Level," *The School Review*, LXX, No. 3 (Autumn, 1962), 303-314.

of diverse pieces of equipment; the improved performance in the field by teachers who had time to plan properly; and by the prevailing mood for learning which team teaching encourages.

The more suspicious members of the teaching profession argue that it is easy to wax eloquent over some new plan for instruction — a plan like the teaching team — simply because it is new. This attitude could disarm the more casual and superficial observer of the true progress of team teaching; however, the more astute observers who have gained much of their knowledge about team teaching in the field of experience are not so easily taken in. They know that the magnetic attraction of team teaching does not lie in its age but in its promise and performance. It offers, for example, many avenues and opportunities not possible in the old traditional method of teaching. This was a discovery made at Wayland High School. In describing this discovery Edward J. Anderson said: "Most important, team teaching has allowed us to introduce a rare ingredient into education. It is free time. . .The whole point of free time is to fill it with responsibilities and have faculty available to guide the children."[5] Who can resist a plan that offers free time to help guide children!

Results of Surveys

Many surveys made of team teaching reveal that on the whole pupils profit, the staff profits, and the school profits. These surveys reveal that practical educators are often reluctant to pinpoint the advantages of team teaching. On the whole they all seem to agree on the advantages, thus a pattern or cluster of advantages appears. The following advantages of team teaching seem to stand out:

1. Although degrees of activity vary, team teaching is feasible if properly organized in all subject areas and on any level of instruction.

2. Valuable integration of important subject matter is possible in team teaching.

3. In a team situation there are opportunities for pupils to develop habits of independent study and self-responsibility.

[5]Edward J. Anderson, "How We Made the Change-Over," *Life Magazine*, LIV, No. 12 (March 22, 1963), 86.

4. In a team teaching project it is much easier to get community resources into the school program since outside guests would be more willing to speak before large groups. It is also more convenient to be able to group the pupils into large groups so all can benefit.

5. The use of aides frees the teacher from burdensome clerical duties so he can plan, devote more time to his students, capitalize on his strengths, and improve his weaknesses, and add variety and stimulation to his teaching techniques.

6. The team is an excellent instrument for in-service education and promoting professional advancement.

7. On the whole, when teachers and pupils work together on a team a feeling of unity develops.

8. The procedures of team teaching improve student discipline and provide for a framework of student expectations.

9. Team teaching provides an opportunity for classroom experimentation via the use of technological devices (projectors, closed circuit television, tape recorders, etc.).

10. Team teaching encourages the expansion in scope of familiar materials, the use of new materials, and helps to discover the weaknesses of an inadequate curriculum.

11. Teachers on a team teaching project live in an "idea-exchange" world which broadens their knowledge through sharing, and develop a teaching group consciousness (as vis-à-vis the old self-contained classroom which militated against this) that is healthy for the school community.

12. The absence of one teacher on a team, if properly organized, will not disrupt the program. This has great implications for both staff utilization and for the substitute teacher program.

13. Team teaching provides career opportunities for professional teachers (may eliminate "plateau-itis" or the cul-de-sac feeling that skilled teachers sometimes acquire after being in the field many years), with possible financial remuneration.

14. Team teaching when planned properly can arrange and provide for the guidance of each of its pupils.

15. Students benefit from the new curriculum devised for team teaching partly because this new curriculum has been broadened and partly because it is more adquately presented by teachers best prepared in the subject area.[6]

16. Team teaching provides for flexible scheduling which frees large blocks of time. Much depends, however, on how this time is used. If it is utilized properly the added saving can be given to

---

[6]"The data indicate that boys on the team were considerably less likely to be referred to counselors for disciplinary action than were boys in non-team classes." Claremont Teaching Team Program, *Annual Report, 1961-62* (Claremont, Calif.: Claremont Graduate School and University Center, 1962), 28.

remedial study groups, working with teaching machines (assisted by an aide), library research, independent study, and seminar groups.

17. Team teaching uses the large-group lecture to advantage (combined knowledge of the teachers and the electronic devices), and the small-group (in seminar study group) in a way not possible in the isolated classroom.

18. Small group instruction so necessary to developing the ability to make decisions and in thinking and planning with others is an integral part of team teaching.

19. Improved staff utilization coupled with improved utilization of building space might eventually reduce school costs. This is, however, not inevitable since much depends upon how the team teaching projection is planned.

20. Under the team teaching plan with its large-group instruction more students can receive instruction without increasing the number of teachers, and remedial and enrichment activities can be facilitated.[7]

21. In team teaching the administrator and the teachers really become partners in the educational enterprise both in theory and in fact, since the planning is done together and in many cases the team leaders may serve as the administrator's council.

22. Team teaching offers the opportunity of expanding the guidance and counseling services since in many cases the counselor is a part of the team, works with the team, and can observe the educational process more closely than he can from the Olympian heights of a closed room.

These are only a few of the advantages of team teaching; there are many others. If team teaching is organized properly and carefully it can produce efficiency and effectiveness and obtain variety and flexibility in the school program. There really is no limit to the possibilities of team teaching, and perhaps this is its greatest advantage. It creates an experimental mood, and teaching becomes a way of manipulating a variety of sources for learning. In short, it does what we all hope sound education should do, and that is encourage the student to assume the responsibility for his own education.

---

[7]"Team teaching especially helps students prepare for a college education. It teaches us how to take notes properly. . . ." "The teacher combinations are so neat that I find myself paying more attention. Alone each teacher is such a good teacher that I learn more." These comments were made by students who indicated they would wish to enroll in a team teaching class another year. Long Beach Unified School District *Report,* Long Beach, Calif., 1962.

We all realize that none of the ideas suggested by team teaching are entirely original or final, and that it will not bring about a change in the role of everyone in the school population. We know now, however, that there is a great amount of merit inherent in the team teaching approach which could lead us to new educational horizons!

Part II

Time for Learning — Experimentation in Scheduling for Learning

Harold Taylor, former president of Sarah Lawrence College, in an address before the Association for Supervision and Curriculum argued that: "The trouble is that the major emphasis among educators is not on changing the system to one which distinguishes among individual children and gives to each the teaching he needs, but on retaining the system and pushing the children through more material faster."[8] Now this is exactly what team teaching does not do. Not only is experimentation in team teaching re-examining the *status quo*, but the many team teaching projects have encouraged educators into new ways and byways of learning.

Technological change and the new educational media undoubtedly call for a better use of school time — perhaps solid blocks which are uninterrupted by the traditional school intrusions. This is the point that Trump makes when he says: "One basic problem concerns the necessary departure from a conventional school schedule. . .A first step in solving this problem is to view time in larger blocks."[9] We see now that the force of tradition and the ease of scheduling, aided and abetted by the constant overshadowing tyranny of the Carnegie Unit, forced many schools into the mold of fixed scheduling.

---

[8]Ward Whipple, "A Report on the ASCD Conference," *Civic Leader*, XXX, No. D29 (April 27, 1964), 3.

[9]J. Lloyd Trump, "Problems Faced in Organizing A School Differently," *The American School Board Journal*, CXLVII, No. 5 (November, 1963), 7. See also L. Weisenberg, "More Time for Teaching: Modular Scheduling," *Ohio Schools*, XLI (December 15, 1963), 14-15, and J. Otterness et al, "Flexible Scheduling in Junior High School," *Minnesota Journal of Education*, XLIV (December, 1963), 19.

Time an Essential Factor in Learning

Using Time Wisely

One of the most important things that a good team teaching project does in any school is examine and attempt to reinvest the school time. In her excellent assay of education and time Helen C. Wood wisely points out that "time is one of the dimensions of opportunity. . .To find and recover more time is to increase opportunity."[10] Here we find the concept of flexible scheduling wedded to team teaching. Team teaching calls for blocks of time fashioned to suit the needs of the teacher, the pupil, and the curriculum area, and to provide the opportunity to plunge into the depths of knowledge rather than simply covering the vague hieroglyphics of some Procrustean outmoded syllabus.

The Extracurriclum Program a Danger

In a good team teaching project which has been well planned we find that "time is a tool used in the learning process rather than an arbitrarily divided dimension."[11] Many schools have "timetable" troubles because by custom, tradition, and sins of omission large blocks of time are lost — wasted away by the intrusion of non-academic matters (often administrative or clerical), and the unfortunate growth of runaway extracurricular programs. Although many educators and administrators are loathe to admit it, this extracurricular program in many of our schools may be symbolized by the voracious, Lola-type enchantress who sings in an off key "What Lola wants, Lola gets." The spirit of this temptress often permeates the entire school, disrupting all normal educational activity. It would be pointless to argue that there is little truth in this indictment. Like all blanket condemnations, the small core

---

[10]Helen Cowan Wood, "Time and Opportunity," *Childhood Education*, XL, No. 7 (March, 1964), 353-56. See also Oscar Jarvis, *Time Allotments and Pupil Achievement in the Intermediate Elementary Grades*, Research Study No. 8 Doctor's Thesis. Houston: Bureau of Education, Research and Services, University of Houston, 1962, 25-60.

[11]E. W. Landis and R. Boston, "Flexible Scheduling: Harbor Beach Community High School," *The Bulletin* of the National Association of Secondary School Principals, XLVII (May, 1963), 79. See also Oscar T. Jarvis, "Time Allotment in Elementary Schools: Policies and Practices," *National Elementary Principal*, XLIII (September, 1963), 64-5, and Herbert E. Phillips, "We Lengthened the School Day," *Phi Delta Kappan*, XLIII, No. 4 (January, 1962), 168-9.

of truth is smothered by exaggeration. Those of us who are concerned with a well-balanced program should be alerted to the danger of time loss in the school.

Time Losses

Too often faculty zeal for the activities and the tangible fruits of student government (and occasionally faculty indifference) produce a situation in which student affairs and campus politics supersede the regular educational program. On the elementary level the holiday programs often serve in place of student or campus affairs. It is a rare high school indeed in which seniors, and other class members, are not able to arrange at will to be excused from classes in order to participate in student activities. In many schools the very plethora of student functions necessarily pushes the academic program into the background.[12]

Dedicated and devoted teachers protest that this could never happen at their school. It *is* being done by the manipulation of a fixed, inflexible daily time schedule wherein "my time becomes your time." This is not to say that the extracurricular program is not a legitimate part of the educational program; on the contrary, the former can be seen to have as long and respectable a history as the more formalized aspects of school life. School for the Athenian youth of the fifth century B.C. was a leisure-time activity, flexibly planned, with the functions of educating him in the intelligent use of his leisure. We have not as yet, in the twentieth-century, provided for such a program. The Greeks considered the best education to consist of esthetic, moral, civic, and physical as well as intellectual education; it is this connotation which the liberal arts tradition, genuinely interpreted, attempts to foster.

Team Teaching Can Help Strike a True Balance

Despite the critics, contemporary curricula which involve concern for leisure time, physical recreation, esthetics, and creative expression are in fact reinforcers of the genuine classical tradition, not departures from it. As in most areas of life and education, here

---

[12]Nicholas C. Polos, "My Time Is Your Time," California Teachers Association *Journal*, LVII, No. 9 (December, 1961), 22.

too a balance must be struck and maintained so that the school life
and shape is in proper proportion. Although a great deal of emphasis has been placed in the recent past on the efficacy of team teaching programs and the programs for the gifted, it is quite obvious
and this is often overlooked, that a solid team teaching program,
carefully organized and tied to a flexible schedule that is indeed
flexible can do much to solve many of the school's problems.[13]
For example, a new time block utilization could plan the school
program so that the extracurricular activities would not interfere
in any way with the educational process, and yet be a reasonable
part of the school day.

New Problems Answered in a New Way

Team teaching necessarily means rescheduling and using time
wisely. This is done in part by the redeployment of teaching talent,
curriculum changes, the breaking up of fixed grade level restric-
tions and time barriers, and in some instances the restructuring of
large segments of the school program. Team teaching planning
even forces some of the traditional school problems into the cold
light of critical review. For example, during the planning stages
a great deal of serious consideration must be given to the methods
of grouping students. What is the best way a team can group 300
pupils for two areas of learning (physics and mathematics), with
a staff of four teachers, two part-time teachers and an aide? This
enterprise raises a host of questions about former practices in education regarding ability grouping, proper sizes of classes, how time
is to be used properly, etc. This is not to say that embarking upon
the high seas of team teaching will easily float the bark of education into havens or bays of safe and comfortable answers. Actually, team teaching will not provide answers for many educational
problems; in many cases it will present many serious challenges
which seem insurmountable.

The New Challenges

These challenges which result from team teaching planning
make education of the young a fascinating pursuit and shed a new

---

[13]Cyril W. Woolcock, "Cautions About Educating Gifted and Talented Students," *The Bulletin* of the National Association of Secondary-School Principals,
XLVII, No. 287 (December, 1963), 11.

light on the problems of how to handle school time, space, large numbers of students, and shifting curriculum.[14] Educators are men and women of intellect, and as such should heed Schopenhauer's sage advice: "Ordinary people think merely how they spend their time; a man of intellect tries to use it."

Flexibility and Team Teaching

Many educators today are interested in new ways which will not only break the grade lockstep and do away with the "egg-crate" type school layout but will also provide for better staff utilization, new methods of organizing for different instruction, and ways to use time more effectively.[15] The *key* word here is flexibility, but flexibility is not the by-product of some organizational plan or method; on the contrary it must purposefully be built into the school curriculum. After a school has carefully examined what Michael calls "the omnibus role of classroom teachers," the advantages of the single subject team or the interdisciplinary team, and the many variables that go into planning for team teaching, then without the haste which has made many schools repeat the same mistakes made in the earlier projects a school should begin to plan their team teaching.[16]

Advantages of Flexible Scheduling

Naturally an important segment of this plan should be concerned with flexible scheduling. There are many advantages in the use of flexible scheduling; however, as always there are some pitfalls which should be avoided. Before any attempt is made to change the scheduling educators should review the objectives of their teaching program. Time of itself has no magic — if changes are to be made in the scheduling of the students then educators should ask themselves — time changes for what? Will this bring

---

[14]See U. B. Ellis and Stanley B. Dick, "Scheduling the Practical and the Fine Arts in the Large Junior High School," *The Bulletin* of the National Association of Secondary-School Principals, XLVI, No. 273 (April, 1962), 36-41.

[15]B. Frank Brown, "The Non-Graded School," *The Bulletin* of the National Association of Secondary-School Principals, XLVII, No. 283 (May, 1963), 64-73; and see Ronald Lippitt, et al, *The Dynamics of Planned Change* (New York: Harcourt Brace & Co., 1958).

[16]Lloyd S. Michael, "Team Teaching," *The Bulletin* of the National Association of Secondary-School Principals, XLVII, No. 283 (May, 1963), 37.

about new curriculum articulation? Will these changes improve the entire development of the student by permitting his shifting from group to group according to his ability or his progress?[17]

Disadvantages of Flexible Scheduling

One large high school developed an intricate flexible schedule for the entire student body with many types of time blocks, and then found that their curriculum was deficient, i.e., not properly planned so there was proper correlation between various segments of the subject areas — in fact there were not even enough electives to make proper use of the time which had been alloted for this purpose. In this instance the entire program had not been correctly reviewed and the attempt to gain time flexibility had not been properly harnessed to the basic school program. This was a situation in which some educator became enamoured with change as a fad and not as a bona fide improvement of the educational program.[18]

THE "DISARMING" INFLUENCE. Another serious pitfall is the "disarming" influence, and this is that many educators often feel that changes in the method of scheduling students will solve their other educational problems. Naturally this is expecting too much, since time manipulation does not decrease student numbers, provide more needed space, or correct a deficient curriculum.

THE PATTERN OF POSSIBLE RIGIDITY. There is also a strong possibility that simply because a school has overhauled the entire schedule, tinkered with it, and made important changes in the time patterns which now provide a form of flexible scheduling the new schedule could in a fairly short time become rigid — as rigid as the old schedule if it is not reviewed from time to time. The pattern of rigidity is not new to education, and there is no magic in flexibility because what was once flexible in any program may soon become inflexible. Like a suit of clothes education often has to be tailored to the student.

[17]See J. Lloyd Trump, "Developing and Evaluating a Class Schedule to Help Each Pupil Learn Better," *Journal of Secondary Education*, XXXVI (October, 1961), 338-45, and B. Frank Brown, "The Non-Graded High School," *Phi Delta Kappan*, XLIV (February, 1963), 206-09.

[18]J. Lloyd Trump, "Flexible Scheduling: Fad or Fundamental?" *Phi Delta Kappan*, XLIV, No. 8 (May, 1963), 367-371.

King Computer — a Panacea

Flexible scheduling today has found an ally — the electronic computer. Here again educators seem to have found solace in refuge in King Computer, as though the electronic machines will mysteriously develop sound educational concepts as underpinning for their educational structures. They suffer from what what Trump calls "machine-panacea," and the author would call "electronic euphoria."[19] With their important data the electronic machines cannot do more than aid in the physical mechanics of flexible scheduling. This is a valuable assistance for modern education, but even such a highly complex program as the SCHED Computer Program (Stanford Computer Help for Educational Development, tested and ready in September, 1964) cannot write the philosophy and objectives of any school program. Nor can it guarantee that simply because the school time is rearranged in time blocks better learning will result.

The Variable Time Factor

There is now, however, enough evidence based upon field research, and substantial projects in progress, to confirm the fact that flexible scheduling properly devised will bring several important advantages to a sound school program. Flexible scheduling, for example, as used in team teaching, will permit academically talented students to enroll in more electives. Instead of the fixed and uniform program you now have the variable time factor as seen in the use of block time, derived from the core-type classes, the use of the floating or rotating period, and the use of the modular schedule (infra), which is the smallest amount of time alloted for instructional purposes. Team teaching uses flexible scheduling to vary the class sizes (small groups and large groups), and provide for independent study. In regard to groups, flexible scheduling provides an important educational advantage. In the scheduling and grouping of pupils in a team Martha W. Bruce writes: "The grouping potentialities of the team are perhaps of the most obvious advantage in the area of individual pupil placement, for the flexibility of the team set-up allows the shifting of

---

[19]J. Lloyd Trump, Ibid.

individuals from group to group, especially at the break between units."[20]

Time to Teach and Learn

Not only can students carry more units or subjects, but they can in many cases proceed at their own speed, do more intensive work in any subject area by departing from the narrow confines of the textbook and also doing independent study. Flexible scheduling permits proper use of teacher specialization, the possibility of the proper guidance and evaluation of pupils, the opportunity for teachers to prepare much better, and the possibility for teachers to provide much sounder programs in the sciences, the social sciences, the vocational arts and the language arts. Once again the use of the team concept in a flexible time atmosphere may present problems, but these can be solved in an atmosphere of shared planning. Seaberg, for example, argues: "The new team member may discover a Malthusian law of team teaching: as the number of teachers increases arithmetically, administrative details increase geometrically."[21]

Administrative Details

Administrative details are an intrinsic part of teaching. The important problem is how to incorporate these into the program properly. Flexible scheduling will provide the teacher more time to handle these details. In a sense team teaching wedded to a sound flexible schedule can provide programs for the gifted and also special attention for the below-average and very slow learner.

In the Pittsburgh Team Teaching Project an effort has been made to find the most potentially able children in each school even though test scores were not always in the superior or gifted range. The team schedule was so arranged that all the children would be given special opportunity for broader and deeper experiences.

The Chapin High School, in Chapin, South Carolina, provides a fine example of flexible scheduling tied to team teaching. At this

20Martha W. Bruce, "Scheduling and Grouping Pupils in A Team," *Civic Leader*, XXX, No. 23 (March 9, 1964), 3.
21.Stanley Seaberg, "Team — But Teach," *Clearing House*, XXXVIII, No. 3 (November, 1963), 168.

MARSHALL HIGH SCHOOL TEACHER PROGRAM 1963-64

NAME ENGLISH TEACHER

REG. ROOM B-42

Per	Time	Monday Course	Rm	Tuesday Course	Rm	Wednesday Course	Rm	Thursday Course	Rm	Friday Course	Rm
Reg.	8:05										
1	8:15	E 5-6 B LAB	B-45	E 5-6 EE LAB	B-42	E 5-6 EE MG	B-28	Team Planning		Activity Period	
2	8:35	E 5-6 B LAB	B-45	E 5-6 EE LAB	B-42	E 5-6 EE MG	B-28	Team Planning		Activity Period	
3	8:55	E 5-6 B LAB	B-45	E 5-6 EE LAB	B-42	E 5-6 EE MG	B-28			Activity Period	
4	9:15	E 5-6 B LAB	B-45	E 5-6 EE LAB	B-42	E 5-6 A LG	A-30	E 5-6 B LAB	B-47	E 5-6 A MG	B-44
5	9:35	E 5-6 A SG	B-46	E 5-6 A LAB	B-49	E 5-6 A LG	A-30	E 5-6 B LAB	B-47	E 5-6 A MG	B-44
6	9:55	E 5-6 A SG	B-46	E 5-6 A LAB	B-49			E 5-6 B LAB	B-47	E 5-6 A MG	B-44
7	10:15	E 5-6 B LG	A-30	E 5-6 A LAB	B-49	E 5-6 A MG	B-16	E 5-6 B LAB	B-47	E 5-6 A LG	A-30
8	10:35	E 5-6 B LG	A-30	E 5-6 A LAB	B-49	E 5-6 A MG	B-16			E 5-6 A LG	A-30
9	10:55	E 5-6 A SG	C-3	E 5-6 B LG	A-30	E 5-6 A MG	B-16	E 5-6 B LG	A-30	E 5-6 A SG	B-27
10	11:15	E 5-6 A SG	C-3	E 5-6 B LG	A-30	E 5-6 A SG	B-40	E 5-6 B LG	A-30	E 5-6 A SG	B-27
11	11:35					E 5-6 A SG	B-40	Lunch			
12	11:55	Lunch		Lunch		Lunch		Lunch		Lunch	
13	12:15	Lunch		Lunch		Lunch				Lunch	
14	12:35	Team Planning								E 5-6 EE SG	B-46
15	12:55			Student Union						E 5-6 EE SG	B-46
16	1:15							Student Conferences			
17	1:35			Supervision		E 5-6 B LG	A-30				
18	1:55	Student Conferences		E 5-6 B SG	B-47	E 5-6 B LG	A-30			E 5-6 B SG	B-45
19	2:15			E 5-6 B SG	B-47					E 5-6 B SG	B-45
20	2:35			E 5-6 A SG	B-56	E 5-6 A SG	B-42	E 5-6 B LG	A-30	E 5-6 A SG	B-42
21	2:55			E 5-6 A SG	B-56	E 5-6 A SG	B-42	E 5-6 B LG	A-30	E 5-6 A SG	B-42
	3:10										

ENGLISH TEAM LEADER

The English department consists of 17 full-time instructors and one half-time intern. The freshman English program is a part of the combined English-social studies department (E 1-2, SS 1-2). Generally, students are scheduled into four levels of classes. (EE) educational enrichment, (A) college capable, (B) average, or (C) remedial English classes. Teaching teams vary from two to five for the required 9-12 English courses.

With the assistance of Portland's *Guide for High School English*, the teaching teams designed the course structure, content, and teaching assignments for each group.

During the weekly cycle, students attend one large-group presentation (80-290 students), one medium group (25-50), one small group (10-18) and one writing lab. (25-50) in the required English courses.

The large-group classes serve to introduce the basic unit or topic which will be pursued for the following week, and to explain assignments, present guest speakers, and stimulate the students to read and discuss the material. Responsibility for large-group presentations is related among team members, and each presenter plans and coordinates the work for the three other groups. In the medium-group sessions, teachers discuss the text, give objective tests, lead the class in discussion and elicit questions from the group. The small group — a most challenging and rewarding experience — gives the students opportunities to present their views of what they have read and studied and to analyze the contributions of others. Some groups use student leaders, and in others the teacher plays the leadership role.

In the writing laboratories, the students coordinate all of their learning from the three other groups. They have time to review the unit, organize their thoughts, and write essays covering the material they have learned both in the classroom and during their independent study time.

A teacher's schedule follows:

The English instructor whose program is presented above is the leader of E 5-6A team of four teachers, a member of the five-instructor team of E 5-6B, and also teaches the E 5-6EE section. Her EE class joins the E 5-6A large-group session for modules 7 and 8 on Fridays. Although one planning session is scheduled during the week for each teaching team, teachers take time for additional planning sessions during and after school.

A teacher's program provides a two-module lunch period, individual student or teacher conference time, two modules per week for supervisory duty in an assigned study hall, and free time to explore new ideas, prepare for classes, or relax. Altogether this teacher is scheduled to teach about 70% of the time.

school the periods are 100 minutes in length, and the classes meet on Monday, Wednesday and Friday, and in the alternate week on Tuesday and Thursday. This new type of scheduling offers better opportunity to give serious consideration to students having difficulties with their studies, expanded curriculum offerings, expanded time for those classes that need it (science, vocational areas, etc.), a type of supervised study period, time for proper guidance and counseling, and more opportunity for extracurricular activities by scheduling the latter properly.[22]

Time and Team Teaching

Team teaching modifies the schedule by taking the time and dividing it into blocks to suit the needs of the subject areas and the type of learning (seminars or independent study). As a rule if team teaching is to operate properly the schedule must be much more flexible than the usual "floating" period or the simple "rotating" period.[23] In order to gain flexibility the school schedule should be prepared to move into a form of block scheduling, i.e., dividing class time into "50, 75, 100, and 150 minutes which are repeated two, three, four or five times a week. . . ."[24]

Computers, Modules and the Team

Robert Bush and Dwight W. Allen together with Robert Oakford are the coordinators of the FAE Computer Technique Project (on flexible scheduling) at Stanford University. They have investigated various types of flexible scheduling including sequence rotation, displaced rotation, compressed rotation and expanded rotation (*supra*).[25]

---

[22]Robert Bush and Dwight W. Allen, "Flexible Scheduling," *The Bulletin* of the National Association of Secondary-School Principals, XLVII, No. 283 (May, 1963), 97.

[23]Edwin F. Clemmer, "The Rotating Schedule at Claremont Junior High School," *The Bulletin* of the National Association of Secondary-School Principals, XLIV, No. 254 (March, 1960), 56-7.

[24]Robert Bush and Dwight W. Allen, *op. cit.*, 79.

[25]Robert Bush and Dwight W. Allen, *op. cit.*, p. 18, and pp. 73-79, provide an excellent, vivid description of various forms of flexible scheduling, with explanations of the team teaching programs and types of scheduling used in our schools.

The Module Concept

Many schools today are using the modular time concept. In most instances the modular concept involves a short unit of time such as 15 or 20 minutes, sometimes larger, and the school day is built by providing a large number of modules. An example of this is to be seen in the illustration following. Claremont High School, Claremont, California, for example, has a 21 module day. Each module is 16 minutes long, and flexibility of its curriculum is increased by providing for a "Trimester" Plan. Trimester comes from *tri* or three and *mensis* or month; the result is a three month block or period of learning. This Plan is proposing that the school year of nine months be broken into three-month periods instead of two standard eighteen week periods. The school year begins and ends as usual (September to June). The change is an internal one within these two natural limits. From a prima facie view it would seem that little is gained in giving time to students and teachers, but a closer view reveals that a great deal could be gained in learning. For example, under this plan it would be possible to teach chemistry or physics or some of the important industrial arts courses two days per week for 120 continuous minutes, and in the long run this is a much better way to teach science than the old fixed 50 minute period each day for five days a week. It is suggested that the vocational arts by this type of planning could sensibly use a larger block of time than now being utilized to develop an understanding in depth and the type of skill needed to achieve satisfaction and ability in this area. In the area of the social sciences the classes could meet three times per week (Monday, Wednesday, and Friday), throughout three twelve week periods rather than daily. Perhaps in this way the student of history will be able to delve into the important matters of history rather than skim the surface and acquire a "bag" of unrelated facts. This is a unique plan which offers a student a flexible daily program, and a flexible school year program. Admitting the fact that there will be some scheduling difficulties (which could be resolved) a student under this plan could take twelve weeks of typing and if that satisfies his need he could then take twelve weeks of sculpturing or music appreciation, and then possibly a twelve week introduction to the history of England. There is really no limit to the possibilities that such a plan offers — and it is made possible only through the use of flexible scheduling. Here the educator is limited only by his imagination, or possibly his resistance to change. This is a program designed to manipulate time as a factor of learning, and this is inevitable if we are to meet the challenges of the twenty-first century.

EXAMPLES OF THE MODULE CONCEPT IN OPERATION. There are many such unique programs which deserve careful examination. Ridgewood High School at Norridge, Illinois, has developed a 21 module (20 minutes) school day, as have Mt. Tacoma High School (Tacoma, Wash.), Brookville High School, Brookville, Kansas), and many others. One of the most unique and revolutionary programs in flexible scheduling is the Brockhurst Junior High School program (Anaheim, California). In this type of planning the teacher determines the time needed for each instructional unit, and the unit of work is completed on a "contract" basis. This is a plan worth examining, probably because it introduces the "pixillation" method, i.e., it introduces animation in learning into already live students![26]

The Road to Better Learning

Favorable acceptance of team teaching does not depend upon the denigration of past educational practices, but upon the application of concepts which result in better learning. The introduction of flexibility into the time scheduling is not intended to facilitate "mass instruction"; on the contrary, it is to improve the quality of our education by the better use of staff organization, encourage students to pursue learning, provide for a feasible and flexible curriculum to meet the challenging world needs, and finally to challenge our youth socially, intellectually, and physically to prepare themselves to be productively engaged in all areas of our democratic American society.

---

[26]Robert Bush and Dwight W. Allen, *op. cit.*, p. 84.

Part III

The Teacher for Tomorrow

Jonathan Swift in his *Gulliver's Travels* described the manner of education children in Lilliput received by writing: "They have certain professors well-skilled in preparing children for such a condition of life as befits the rank of their parents, and their own capacities, as well as inclinations."[27] Whether Swift realized it or not he put his finger on the "triangle of education," — the well-skilled teacher, the student's capacity, and the student's inclination. It would be wonderful but perhaps not so inspiring if education were so simple, but "education" is an elusive and sometimes amorphous thing. Philip Melancthon once argued that the education of the young was more difficult than storming Troy!

In the Graeco-Roman world, as in civilizations prior to that time, much that passed for education was transmitted via the abstract symbols of the culture. In the Middle Ages the rise of the universities tended to mold the written and verbal symbols into a stiff, formalized education. This was buttressed by such traditions and customs as the "society of the scholars," the investiture, and the "laying on of hands." The mold and mode of education hardened and remained fixed for many years. It is impossible to imagine how many countless boys and girls were forced into this academic Procrustean framework!

Some Roots of Educational Development

Education at any given time or place is in large measure the product of the civilization of which it is a part. The changes in society brought about by the humanism of the Renaissance, the Age of Discovery, and the subsequent enlightenment had a deep, profound influence upon education and its methods.

The process was slow but the influence of the naturalism of Rousseau which led to Pestalozzi's experiments at Burgdorf and Yverdun soon bore fruit. The insistence upon direct experiences for the child instead of the continued use of verbal and written

---

[27]Jonathan Swift, *Gulliver's Travels* (Reading, Pa.: The Spencer Press, 1937), 35.

symbols was still, however, rare in both America and Europe. The isolated examples of educational experiments with methods were suspect at that time. The emphasis upon science and the emergence of the theory of evolution resulted in what J. B. Bury called "the age of progress." These changes had a profound effect in the twentieth century upon educational theory and educational philosophy.

Challenge of the Present

Since the turn of the century many new methods have been developed, and it appeared that finally there was "something new under the sun." In recent years, for example, it appeared that the American dream of education was reaching its fullest realization; public school enrollment grew to over 35 million in 1960. It quickly became obvious to most Americans that the "little red schoolhouse" methods of education were now obsolete. This was the kind of progress in education that other civilizations had not enjoyed. Such rapid progress, however, brought problems which seemed insurmountable.

Teacher Shortage

One of the most important questions which plagued American education in the mid-twentieth century, and indeed still does, was how to obtain first-rate teachers to staff a large institutionalized system of education. For example, between the opening of classes in fall 1959 and the corresponding date in 1960, "a total of 116,100 classroom teachers in the public elementary and secondary schools left the teaching profession. This number represented 8.1 per cent of the total teaching staff in those schools at that time."[28]

It was this severe teacher shortage situation, in part, which gave such great impetus to team teaching programs, for the heart of such programs is inevitably a deep concern for proper staff utilization.

---

[28]Frank Lindenfeld, *Teacher Turnover in Public Elementary and Secondary Schools, 1959-60*, Circular No. 675, OE-23002-60 (Washington, D. C.: U. S. Dept. of Health, Education, and Welfare, 1963), 7.

The Preparation of the Modern Teacher

Another problem in American education which has recently come under fire is the method of preparing the novice teacher. Recent studies such as James D. Koerner's *The Miseducation of American Teachers* and James B. Conant's *The Education of American Teachers* have brought about a re-examination of teacher training methods in the United States. In essence, Conant's argument is that the system of teacher certification by which states dictate what courses a potential teacher must take in college to get a public-school license is poor; and that the end result is an uneducated teacher. He argues that the state rules should be abolished, and that colleges should be free to upgrade teacher training and make classroom performance the test of certification. With good reason many of Conant's critics respond that some colleges may not be responsible enough to uphold high standards on their own.

There is little doubt that today we need a teacher education program that can meet the changing times. The impact of technological change and the explosion of vast areas of knowledge call for a new teacher, one prepared to meet the exigencies of the modern world. The era of the traditional teacher is gone. Charles Dickens, who was in a sense an educational reformer of some merit was merciless in his criticism of the pedantic methods of teaching and learning. One cannot help but chuckle at his description of Gradgrind, the fact-finder. Dickens wrote: "And Gradgrind, as he surveyed the children, seemed a kind of cannon, loaded to the muzzle with facts, and prepared to blow them clean out of the regions of childhood at one discharge."

The Role of the Modern Teacher

Perhaps we may have gone to another extreme today from the Gradgrind to the modern teacher whose principal function is vague and undefined. R. M. Bossone argues that: "Like Camus' Frenchman in *The Stranger,* the teacher is pervaded by a vagueness and uncertainty about himself which is frustrating and appalling."[29] William C. Kvaraceus deplores the fact that the teach-

---

[29] R. M. Bossone, "Teacher's Dilemma," *Peabody Journal of Education,* XLI (September, 1963), 91. For an excellent symposium on Teacher Education see "Focus on Teacher Education," *California Teachers Association Journal,* LX, No. 3 (May, 1964), 3-45.

er's principal function seems to be one of "orchestrating class-room hardware." At any rate we have no alternative today but to take a long, hard look at the present methods of teacher preparation if we are to create the teacher of tomorrow.

Team teaching has great need for leaders who are primarily *educated* men and women. Teachers who have been professionally trained and liberally educated, and thus can staff schools that can develop "cosmopolitan human beings," will need to rid themselves of any kind of regional provincialism, ethnocentricity or prejudice.

Team Teaching and Liberal Preparation

Team teaching is an excellent vehicle for interdisciplinary com-binations of knowledge. This is why it is important that the teacher of tomorrow obtain a broad background of general knowl-edge. In the past the teacher was trained to perform as an isolated individual; the premium was placed upon independence. In the future, however, the emphasis will be placed not upon individual teaching performance but upon the "collective abilities" of teach-ers. The self-contained classroom is in reality a myth, and not at all suited to the needs of tomorrow's citizens.

In the future "bell-less" school society teachers will live an en-tirely different professional life. They will have to be skilled in the use of a variety of teaching techniques, in the use of the new electronic equipment that the technological age is bringing into the classroom, in new methods of planning and sharing responsi-bility for the curriculum, and in general in an ability to work well together in groups. These necessities are implied in most of the team teaching programs, and indeed, are dictated by the changes which are fast becoming a part of our general educational pat-tern of staff obligations. In short teachers need to be prepared to work on a team!

In the future, and this may sound like a form of lese majesty, it may not matter whether all schools or any schools have team teaching programs. What is important for American education is that the teacher of tomorrow be educated and prepared so that he can perform in an atmosphere of "shared responsibility." Then he will be flexible and can fit into any plan of group teaching.

Course Preparation for Team Teaching

Some institutions of higher learning have already taken steps to provide instruction in this direction. The University of California at Los Angeles, Extension Division, provides a course titled "Team Teaching and Staff Utilization (X 320.5(2)." The course description reads: "Existing patterns of team teaching; large and small group instruction, and independent study. Communication and delegation of teaching responsibilities. Use of consultant help. Determination of types of teams possible and desirable. Evaluation of team teaching. Team effort of the administrator, counselor, and teacher. Effective use of interns, helpers, and automated devices."[30]

California State College on Team Teaching

California State College in Los Angeles, California, began a program to prepare teachers suited to team arrangements. The basic premise of the college is that: "Teacher education through team teaching is an additional means of providing better qualified teachers for the schools of today."[31] One might also add that this could be a means of providing better teachers for the schools of tomorrow! The plan of the college is a simple, pilot-type design. It includes four class groups (30-35), large interclass lecture (about 100) groups, discussion groups, and individual student instructor conferences (counseling and advisement). There is a steering committee of three students, one from each class, to assist the professor in the planning and the evaluation of class activities. This was a pioneer effort which should be expanded into an integral part of teacher preparation all over the country.

Team Teaching Aids the Beginning Teacher

Another important segment of teacher preparation is the "incipient phase" of the beginning teacher. This early training period in the field often marks the teacher and sets a pattern which he

---

[30]University Extension *Bulletin,* University of California at Los Angeles (Spring, 1964), 90.

[31]Jack L. Nelson and Gertrude A. Robinson, "Teacher Education Through Team Teaching," *School and Society,* XCI, No. 2234 (December 14, 1963), 409-10. See University of Maine, Orono, Maine, Program.

will follow later in his professional life. Actually the idea of a "team" is really a boon to a beginning teacher.[32] A new teacher lives in a world of confusion, anxiety, and urgency. The team, if properly structured and not thrown hastily together, provides a highly organized framework within which the new teacher can continue to learn the mysteries of the art of teaching. Here the neophyte finds some form of security and flexibility, an opportunity to learn to share in planning, time to do sensible planning, observe the methods of experienced colleagues, learn how to avoid the pitfalls of inexperienced teaching, receive valuable advice on the matters of discipline, grading, the handling of large and small groups, and how to be a "team" member — in short the team concept helps to build a foundation upon which the beginning teacher can stand firmly.

J. B. Conant on Teacher Preparation

In his book *The Education of American Teachers*, James B. Conant proposed that principals use team teaching as a means of inducting the new teacher into the teaching of his subject. His four-member team would consist of two senior teachers, a third or fourth year probationary teacher, and a beginning teacher. He argues for a four-year period of induction into the teaching profession, and claims that: "During the first year, the beginner is a very junior member of the team, in the fourth year a senior junior so to speak, and almost on par with the teachers who hold a permanent appointment. It is my contention that these four years of induction are also probationary years. The teacher is being educated and assessed." Conant's point here is that if the teacher is not successful this probationary period would serve as a weeding-out process. During the important four-year probationary period which would naturally culminate in a permanent appointment and an increase in salary the new teacher can observe excellent teaching, become familiar with the school's special problems, and learn the "technology" of education, i.e., audio-visual aids, school business methods, etc.

---

[32]Judith von Daler, "The Team: A Boon to the Beginning Teacher," *The Civic Leader*, XXXIII, No. 27 (April 13, 1964), 3.

A New Pattern of Preparation

The teacher of tomorrow will have to learn how a team works and understand his role and the role of the other members of a team. The way many teachers are prepared today, it would be impossible for them to assume "team" responsibilities unless some form of in-service training were given prior to beginning the teaching career. In the new pattern of education the *modus operandi* of the new school will be entirely different — almost like living in a magical world of flexible scheduling, diverse curriculum patterns, aided and abetted by instructional materials and supplies never seen before in the twentieth century! It will have to be a world of shared human compatibility because these changes are, in part, dictated by the dynamics of team teaching and by the many changes which will result from our concentrated research in science and education.

The Respect for Individual Differences

Slowly we have finally come to the realization that teachers are not alike; that they are not interchangeable parts like wheels or cogs in a machine, and that teaching is really an art. Team teaching respects these differences by incorporating the various strengths of teachers. If the teacher of tomorrow is prepared and educated differently he therefore can make the contribution to the school of the future which will adequately serve the needs of society. In this sense team teaching is a promise of commitment.

Summary

There are many possibilities and inherent advantages in team teaching. In a sense team teaching is not an isolated phenomena, but instead really touches on every phase of the school's life, even the extracurricular program. It has not been definitely shown as yet that team teaching conclusively aids learning or that it is the highway of the future; however, there are optimistic signs that team teaching does offer many avenues and opportunities not possible in the old traditional method of "keeping school." There has been enough experimentation at present to show that if team teaching is organized properly it can produce both variety and flexibility in the school program. There is really no limit to the possibilities of team teaching, and perhaps this is its greatest advantage.

Team teaching has helped to expand the experimental mood of American education and this has led to a willingness to use "time as one of the dimensions of opportunity." In this sense educators are now willing to re-examine their traditional use of time — to embark upon new plans to reschedule the school day in order to increase the flexibility of the program which team teaching often dictates. In doing this the educator has shown a willingness to harness the electronic computer to the needs of education.

Team teaching uses flexible scheduling to vary class sizes (small and large groups), and to provide for independent study. There is little doubt that this approach will present a host of problems, but these can be apportioned and solved in an atmosphere of shared planning.

There are many types of flexible scheduling and none fit every school situation. After careful examination of sequence rotation, displaced rotation, and other types of time rotation the school should decide on the basis of their philosophy and objectives which type best fits their needs.

The rise of the modular concept — a block of time allied with a group of students — changes the traditional form of the school day and relates time to learning. Here time is manipulated as a factor in learning in sharp contrast to the old Procrustean 50 or 60 minute period.

Team teaching has a great need for leaders who are primarily *educated* men and women. The future teacher will live an entirely different professional life, and this means that he will have to be prepared to cope with new ideas in flexible scheduling, diverse curriculum patterns, and new instructional materials not used in the past. Only in this way will the teacher of tomorrow be able to keep his commitment to society.

Topics for Discussion and Study

1. Explain how team teaching can be used to influence the extra-curricular program.
2. Why do you think many teachers would be happier in a team situation while some would find it unpleasant or uncomfortable?

3. Explain the various ways in which team teaching can stimulate learning.
4. Describe how it is possible the staff, pupils, and the school program may profit from a solid team project.
5. Do you feel that the advantages as listed are realistic and that team teaching really provides opportunity for variety and flexibility in learning?
6. Why is it so necessary to re-examine the use of school time today?
7. If "time is not an arbitrarily divided dimension" then how would you consider it a tool in the learning process?
8. Explain some of the disadvantages of flexible scheduling.
9. Do you think it is possible for a new flexible schedule to become fixed and rigid in a fairly short time?
10. Explan why better learning will not automatically follow a revised schedule of the school day.
11. Describe accurately the following: sequence rotation; displaced rotation; compressed rotation and expanded rotation. [For example see Robert Bush and Dwight W. Allen, "Flexible Scheduling," NASSP **Bulletin**, XLVII, No. 283 (May, 1963), 97.]
12. What is meant by the "modular" concept? Do you think that this concept will revolutionize time allotment in the school day?
13. Explain the events which have led to a severe teacher shortage in the United States. How would you solve this shortage?
14. Describe the advantage of using team teaching to prepare the novice teacher. Would you propose a different plan to prepare interne teachers?
15. Discuss the important reasons for undertaking an entirely new program for the preparation of the teachers of tomorrow.

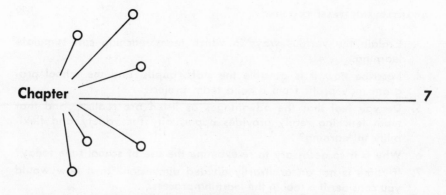

Chapter 7

EDUCATION FOR THE TWENTY-FIRST
CENTURY

When the cold war moved into outer space, the American people became more disturbed than ever about education. "No other people," writes Henry Steele Commager, "ever demanded so much of education as have the American people. None other was served so well by its schools and education."[1] Many critics of American education forgot this when the classrooms became the launching platforms for the futuristic contest for the moon. They argued that Americans are undereducated, overentertained, and that now they are tossing easefully but restlessly in what Reinhold Neibuhr calls a state of "sophisticated vulgarity." Those who remain calm amidst this confusion agree with Henri Peyre, of Yale University, who argues: "On few subjects does it seem harder to keep a level head than the comparison of a country's educational system with that of another land. Criticism to be sure, is the life-blood of the teaching profession. . .But masochistic self-incrimination such as America has indulged in lately. . .is equally ridiculous."[1] Meeting the challenge of the nuclear age will not be easy because of the cries of the detractors, who seem to have lost sight of the fact that a country's educational system reflects the basic values and goals of a society.

Peyre's justifiable point of view did not change the feeling of uneasiness that Americans felt, indeed still feel, about the results

---

[1] Henry Steele Commager, "Our Schools Have Kept Us Free," National Education Association *Journal* (January, 1951), 18-19.

of their educational system. It is a feeling based in part on a sense of urgency. This feeling of urgency and inadequacy has resulted in confusion in education. The self-styled experts are attacking the school systems, their curricula, the teachers, administrators, the emphasis on "life-adjustment" programs, and are even putting total blame on the schools for the social ills of the times.

Problems of Education

In the meantime, serious problems — solutions of which require teamwork among educators and the American people — continue to harass the schools. Overcrowded classes, double sessions, too few fully qualified teachers, inadequate salaries, and other real questions demand attention.

A short time ago B. Frank Brown wrote: "The bravery with which schools introduce new heresies can be compared to the quavering whistle of a man taking a short cut through a cemetery at midnight in the dark of the moon. We must take care that promising new heresies do not become dull new orthodoxies."[2] This may have been true at one time, but today Americans are trying to respond creatively to changing needs and circumstances. In fact the changing needs and the challenge of the space age have already hastened the demand for quality in education and for new methods of instructional staff organization, and has placed strong emphasis on the discovery and stimulus of our talented students.

A Series of Revolutions

No, we are not suffering today from the malady of "chronic and excessive caution." Jerome S. Bruner, codirector of the Center for Cognitive Studies at Harvard University, has described the dimensions of three modern simultaneous revolutions in American education as follows: (1) a revolution in the nature of a book; (2) a revolution in the shape and content of curriculum; and (3) a revolution in the image of the learning process.[3] The complexity of

---

[2]B. Frank Brown, "A New Design for Individual Learning," *Journal of Secondary Education*, XXXVIII, No. 6 (October, 1962), 369.

[3]Quoted from "ATPI: Progress Report on Changes in Educational Materials." Jerome S. Bruner, "Revolution in the Concept of A Book," *Publisher's Weekly*, CLXXXI (April 30, 1962), 12-14.

modern problems in education demands unprecedented, many-sided solutions, and these depend in part on the nature of the changes.

Americans are not averse to change in education. Alistair Cooke said in 1952, "America may end in spontaneous combustion, but never in apathy, inertia or uninventiveness." Over the many years with cautious optimism we have tried the Gary Plan, the Pueblo Plan, the Platoon School, the Winnetka Plan, the Dalton Plan, Hosic's Cooperative Group Plan (a multiple-platoon system), and the recent Dual Progress Plan. There is a great deal of truth in D. C. McClelland's statement that "Americans have already discovered, and are pursuing with alarming vigor, a system for encouraging excellence."[4] We are searching for excellence on every level of our national life.

Search for Excellence

In this constant search we often accept change simply because it is something different. Sometimes we are caught up in the pressures of the times. Team teaching, for example, is now in its early stages of development, and although there is the ethos of an educational reform movement the process of development cannot be accelerated without research and proper experimentation. This is made quite clear in the recent Norwalk Plan *Fourth Report*, which stated: "Internally certain modifications in staff utilization and pupil programs will continue to be necessary to strengthen the team teaching organization. . .Where there is favorable evidence of good practices in team teaching more will be sought. Where the program has shown signs of weakness, efforts will be made to be more effective."[5] Here is a bona fide effort to take into consideration the many factors which impinge upon team teaching. This is the type of field research which avoids faddism and capricious shifts based on "single research studies of doubtful validity."

---

[4]David C. McClelland, "Encouraging Excellence," Stephen R. Graubard and Gerald Holton, ed., *Excellence and Leadership in A Democracy* (New York: Columbia University Press, 1962).

[5]*The Norwalk Plan of Team Teaching, Fourth Report, 1962* (Norwalk, Conn.: Norwalk Board of Education, 1962), p. 24. See also Lester W. Anderson, "Countdown in Education," University of Michigan School of Education *Bulletin*, XXXIV, No. 7 (April, 1963), 101.

Change in American Education

In a recent study edited by Matthew B. Miles of Teachers College (Columbia University) Horace Mann-Lincoln Institute of School Experimentation, the conclusion reached in this 689-page report was that American schools rarely adopt "new ideas for their educational value. Such changes, it is maintained, usually come about through responses to pressures, conformity of new practices to favored ideologies, persuasive claims by salesmen and lobbyists, somebody's intuition, sentiment, and 'messianic zeal.' "[6] The report deals primarily with analysis of how various forces influence the introduction of ideas and practices in schools and colleges. In the past it has been true that changes were not quickly adopted by American schools and that external forces were often responsible for these changes; however, there has been a lessening of resistance to change itself in recent years, and many school systems have shown a willingness to experiment without any external pressure. Perhaps the schools have been made aware of Francis Bacon's admonition: "He that will not apply new remedies must expect new evils; for time is the greatest innovator."

This brings us to the question of the future of team teaching. If we recognize that education has to a great extent become institutionalized in America then we must recognize that team teaching cannot be evaluated in a vacuum.[7] If staff reorganization is the prime objective of team teaching then we have here a procedural method of instruction which does not alter the basic problems of instruction. The problems of curriculum, adequacy of budgets, teacher competency, adequate time for planning and scheduling, and the proper size of instructional groups must all be taken into consideration if team teaching is to proceed in a satisfactory manner. The quality of education is not improved simply by grouping several teachers together.

In his *Paradox and Promise*, H. S. Broudy points out: "The most revolutionary educational proposal of the twentieth-century was that the school and all its personnel, from pupils to administrators,

---

[6]See "Education and Change," *Scholastic Teacher,* LXXXIV, No. 11 (April 17, 1964), 1.

[7]William E. Drake, "Some Implications of the Institutionalization of American Education," History of Education *Quarterly,* I, No. 1 (March, 1961), 41.

be committed to the method of intelligence."[8] In a sense this means that team teaching must go beyond a structural function in a school organization. Its goals and philosophy will have to be refined so that it becomes an intrinsic part of the instructional program. Perhaps new courses will have to be structured and new instructional equipment devised which will complement the efficacy of the team teaching project.

"Open System of Education"

An educator's response to a changing society should include more than a concern for excellence; it should embody the all-inclusive concern that all young people fulfill their potentialities. We know that the socioeconomic status of the student is in part responsible for the educational opportunities which he can enjoy.[9] The school has not always been too successful in counteracting this disadvantage but perhaps a new method of instruction which rearranges the school time and the school curriculum, such as team teaching, may provide a new and different school experience. In the world of tomorrow we will have to base our educational philosophy not on cherished myths but on objective facts. We need to place great emphasis on what Harold H. Anderson, research professor of psychology at Michigan State University, calls "the open system of education." It is Anderson's opinion that the "open system of education," in sharp contrast to the "closed system of education," (memorization, storing of information, etc.) "will encourage original thinking, and break the traditional bonds which hamper creative and imaginative flights toward excellence."[10] Team teaching lends itself to experimentation which may encourage the creativity that we wish to stimulate. There is little doubt but that team teaching projects may lead education to new horizons, and even do much to give some of education's perpetual problems a new perspective.

---

[8]Henry S. Broudy, *Paradox and Promise* (Englewood Cliffs, N. J.: Prentice-Hall, Inc., 1961), 166. See also Fred Hechinger, *The Big Red Schoolhouse* (New York: Doubleday and Co., 1959).

[9]See W. Lloyd Warner, Robert J. Havighurst, and Martin B. Loeb, *Who Shall Be Educated?* (New York: Harper and Bros., 1944), 60-61.

[10]On Experiments on Excellence see Arthur D. Morse, *Schools of Tomorrow-Today* (New York: Doubleday & Co., 1960), Chapt. VI.

Team Teaching and School Problems

The literature of education is replete with suggestions, analyses, and the result of experiments in regard to the superior or the gifted student. Little is written about the "slow learner" or low achiever, and although the dropout has become a familiar figure in educational literature few solutions to these two pressing educational problems have been found.[11] There is no easy answer, and one must subscribe to Mallery's dictum that: "The school must give the student an intellectual challenge to come into action as a sensitive, thinking, feeling individual."[12]

Obviously the team teaching plan or project will not solve all our educational ills and it would be foolhardy to contend that it would do so, but the dynamics of team teaching are such that there are great possibilities for vital change. Whether by design or otherwise, the net effect of sweeping criticisms of American public education has been to undermine the confidence of citizens in their schools. Team teaching projects properly publicized will help to achieve better public understanding of our problems and encourage support for the clearly demonstrable needs of the public schools.

Organic Growth of Education

Team teaching programs will reveal that it is foolhardy to import a few detached features of any foreign educational system and attempt to graft these to our educational framework. Any coherent educational theory and practice mirror the history of a country, its haphazard and yet organic growth of appendages, its ability to devise solutions as expediency requires them, its ideals, and its will to mold the kind of citizens it desires in a particular geographical and political context. Team teaching is an approach in education which tries to solve our problems in our own way within the framework of our historical context.

---

[11]See Charles S. Lewis, "What Makes Sammy Fail?" The *Bulletin* of the National Association of Secondary-School Principals, XLVII, No. 281 (March, 1963), 147-153.

[12]David Mallery, *High School Students Speak Out* (New York: Harper and Row, 1962), 159.

Part II

A New Horizon for Education

Everyone recalls the majestic exordium of Webster's reply to Hayne:

> Mr. President when the mariner has tossed for many days in thick weather . . . he naturally avails himself of the first pause in the storm, . . . to take his latitude and ascertain how far the elements have driven him from his true course.[13]

The time has come to chart the true course of American education.

In the nineteenth century United States the political and economic patterns of life began to overshadow the religious as claimants upon the loyalties and energies of men. The United States was becoming a secular society in which religious institutions still played a strong part but no longer the leading role. This shift in power did not take place without bitter struggles and much searching of the hearts and minds of men.[14]

The growth of political democracy, the expanding role of government, and the growth of nationalism contributed to the concept of public education that took root and flourished despite strong opposition from many quarters. The establishment of schools upon a politico-economic basis, and not a religious basis, was a growth of the nineteenth century.

Many of the gains of the nineteenth century were consolidated in the twentieth century, but in the huge educational undertaking of America gaps began to appear between ideals and their realization, complicated by the explosion brought about by the educational problems brought on by the space age.

The fairly recent invasion of space places entirely new demands on our complete educational processes. In the recent past we have not been able to catch up with the nuclear age, and our educational content, methods, and even objectives have been dictated by the needs of a bygone society to which we cannot return.

It is the responsibility of American education to prepare citizens for tomorrow, and the implications of the constantly chang-

---

13Lindsay Swift, ed., *The Great Debate* (New York: Houghton Mifflin Co., 1898), 11.
14Neil G. McCluskey, *Public Schools and Moral Education* (New York: Columbia Univ. Press, 1958), 260; and William K. Dunn, *What Happened to Religious Education?* (Baltimore: The Johns Hopkins Press, 1958), 308-09.

ing present make this responsibility seem overwhelming. "How," Margaret Mead asked, "are we who do not know what to do, who do not know how to live in one world, who have no faintest trace of habituated capacity to operate in a world which may actually destroy itself, . . . how shall we, who are unfit, prepare a generation which will begin to be fit to face the new problems which confront mankind!"[15] This is the crux of the issue to be determined for the future.

The False Cure-all

Many of the more naive and overly-optimistic educators have conducted a continual search, over a long period of time, for a magical curative agent — a simple formula — a panacea if you will — which would solve all the educational ills. Although many educators have seized upon team teaching as "the road to Utopia," and many have followed these Pied Pipers of Education blindly — it would be wise to enter this caveat. Team teaching will not solve your basic educational problems, i.e., budget difficulties, exploding school population, teacher shortage, and school management problems, and as a matter of fact it may even complicate your present school situation. Team teaching offers a new horizon, but this horizon will become a mirage if it is not properly planned. Stanislau Lec, the Polish writer, once warned the twentieth century by saying: "Watch out that someone else's emotion does not grip your throat!"[16]

Team teaching attracts and stimulates but it also raises many questions which are still unanswered and leaves darkness in some important corners of education. This concept should, however, cause many of us to reconsider the many procedures in education which we have been taking for granted for so many years.

Sidney Harris argues that an educated man is "one who realizes the implications of his beliefs." He is implying here that the storage of facts is a barren education unless there is the lightning interplay of meaning in the constant usage of these facts. This means

---

[15]Quoted in Lewis Paul Todd, "Revising the Social Studies," *Teachers Notebook in Social Studies* (New York: Harcourt Brace and World, Inc., Fall, 1962), 2.

[16]J. M. Hill, of the Superintendent's Office of the San Francisco School District wrote to the author that: "San Francisco has no organized district-wide plan for team teaching." March 25, 1963.

that education for the future will call for continuous interdisciplinary curriculums, and it is suggested that team teaching lends itself very well as a weapon for smashing the high walls of isolated disciplines of knowledge. Perhaps then we will be able to achieve the goal of C. P. Snow and make "scientists out of our humanitarians, and humanitarians out of our scientists."

Unknown Factors in Team Teaching

The introduction of team teaching presents many difficulties. Team teaching is a strange structure built of old and new planks. Many of these forms evade description and remind one of the story of the elephant and the three blind men. It is still too early to evaluate team teaching precisely, primarily because it is still in its foundational period; however, it is not too early to come to grips with the questions raised which must be answered in order to determine the best roads toward the goal of improved learning. Sometimes asking the right questions is much more important than attempting to supply feeble answers. These are questions which must be found in continuous research and whose answers should be applicable to team teaching projects.

Some of the questions which should be explored further if team teaching is to increase its effectiveness are:

1. What are the definite advantages of flexible grouping of students?
2. How does team teaching really affect methods of instruction?
3. What tests must we devise, and how, so that we can accurately measure how students benefit from team teaching?
4. What new courses of study will we need (including new materials such as revised textbooks, electronic equipment, etc.) so that team teaching will be more effective?
5. What are the long-range advantages of team teaching for teachers?
6. How do we handle faculty relationships in a school that is partly committed to team teaching?
7. How are we going to develop materials and techniques for large-group instruction?
8. What is the best way to prepare teachers for the team teaching program?
9. What happens to the gifted student and the slow learner in a team teaching program?

10. What is the best method to institutionalize the concept of "the hierarchy of levels" as a form of merit consideration?

11. What is the best role of the administrator in team teaching?

12. What is the best way to group students for effective team teaching?

13. What is the best way to overcome the difficulties of scheduling, especially in a school which has a partial team teaching program?

14. Will team teaching work in all subject areas, and if so, how? How can team teaching be used in vocational areas?

15. Is team teaching disadvantageous to children in elementary levels? On secondary levels?

16. What is the best way to handle the complex problem of human relationships in teaching teams?

17. How can team teaching best be used with small groups? With seminar sessions, in laboratory situations, and in teaching areas outside of the classroom (Physical Education, for example)?

18. How is team teaching to be financed, as a short-range program or long-range program?

19. How does the team obtain adequate time for planning and evaluation?

20. What is the proper role of the team leader?

21. What is the proper role of the teacher aide?

22. How does team teaching affect the "unmotivated" and meet the emotional needs of children?

23. How can team teaching help in the professional training and growth of future teachers?

24. In a team teaching program what is adequate guidance and counseling support? What is the role of the counselor?

25. What are the "human considerations" of team teaching, i.e., the impact of teacher members, students, nonteam members, parents, the public image of the school, etc?[17]

These are only a few of the important questions raised by team teaching. There are many others which also deserve consideration. The fact of the matter is that team teaching may not be the only answer for tomorrow but may be only *one* of the ways to proceed toward the new horizon.

Need for Precision in Team Teaching Planning

One thing is certain however: team teaching as an instrument for organized instruction needs to be refined into a sharper weapon.

---

[17]See Arthur R. King, Jr., "Planning for Team Teaching: The Human Considerations," *California Journal of Secondary Education*, XXXVII, No. 6 (October, 1962), 362-67.

The results of any team teaching program depend upon what the team does, with whom, for what purpose, and under what conditions. If we continue to experiment with team teaching programs (and there is no doubt that this type of program should be expanded) then through a series of continuous experiments it may be possible to sharpen the image of team teaching and thus increase its usefulness. In this regard Brownell and Taylor offer sound and excellent advice. They suggest: "We recommend close analysis of assumptions, more explicit models, better research design, and more penetrating evaluation of results of team experimentation so that schoolmen will be able to make sound judgements about teaching teams."[18]

It is both necessary and proper for schools to seek ways in which education can help resolve the problems of the twenty-first century.[19] Experimentation with new interpersonal relationships in teaching and learning are inevitable, especially if we are to meet the challenge of change and break out of our present traditional cells which have confined education.[20] This kind of experimentation will mean drastic changes in curriculum. It will mean that the schools are willing to risk the uncertain outcomes of new methods and that team teaching may become a means and not an end in itself. In short, we need to follow Frederick Mayer's advice for the future. In an inspirational suggestion he says that: "What is needed is to dream boldly and then to apply these dreams to the realities of our institutional system."[21]

Naturally, we are all concerned with the overshadowing needs of today, and each of us may have a different conception of the needs for the future. The basic common denominator for us all, however, is that we have visions and ideals and the sense of professional commitment which will implement these ideals.

---

[18]John A. Brownell and Harris A. Taylor, "Theoretical Perspectives for Teaching Teams," *Phi Delta Kappan*, XLIII (January, 1962), 157.

[19]See Frank B. Lindsay, "The American High School After A Decade of Challenge — The Setting for an Appraisal," *California Journal of Secondary Education*, XXXVII, No. 6 (October, 1962), 341-46.

[20]A challenging article on the future is Harry A. Fosdick's, "Flexibility and New Ideas for the Years Ahead," California Teachers Association *Journal* (May, 1963), 42-46.

[21]Frederick Mayer, "The Foundation Is Laid: Now We Need to Build the Structure," California Teachers Association *Journal* (May, 1963), 22.

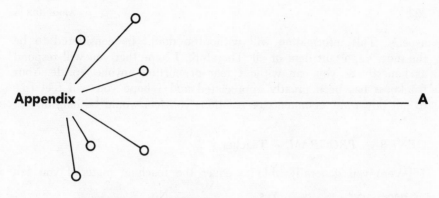

Appendix ──────────────────────────────── **A**

THE QUESTIONNAIRE — AN ATTEMPT AT
EVALUATION

Team teaching is a departure from the traditional program, and as such it is necessary to obtain the views of the many groups influenced by it. There is also the matter of sound public relations which assists in interpreting the image of the school and the objectives of the new program.

Schools are quite skilled at the "questionnaire" procedure, or should be since this is an integral part of the informational source of a school program. The full panoply of questionnaires includes: a teachers' attitude survey; a survey for teachers not included in the team teaching project; a survey or questionnaire for parents whose children are participating in the team program; a survey for parents whose children are not participating in the team teaching program; a questionnaire for administrators; a questionnaire for pupils in the program; and possibly a questionnaire for pupils not in the team teaching program.

The following is a sample of a teacher and pupil questionnaire. This questionnaire is only an indicator of certain attitudes, and should be accepted as such.

TEAM TEACHING EVALUATION*

Name ....

Team ....

This questionnaire has been developed to get your reaction to the general program of team teaching as well as to a number of specific

────────────────────

*Sample questionnaire used by the Mt. Diablo Unified School District. "The Mechanics for eliciting pupil and teacher reaction was probably our most significant contribution to the profession." See H. R. Wall and Robert W. Reasoner, *Team Teaching* (Concord, Calif., 1962), 128-131.

aspects. This information will without a doubt be considered to be the most important data of all. Therefore, I hope that you will respond as honestly as you can without fear of hurting anyone's pride. Your frankness has been greatly appreciated and I hope you will feel free to put down any comments or reactions you feel would be helpful.

GENERAL PROGRAM – Teacher

1. Were you generally able to cover the teaching material you felt necessary?   Yes ....   No ....

2. How did the program for the children on your team compare with what you would have given them if you had them in a self-contained classroom?

   Better program .... About the same .... Poorer program ....

3. Do you feel that you have been able to become sufficiently acquainted with the children in your homeroom?

                    Yes ....   No ....

4. Do you feel a beginning teacher would find it easier or more difficult to work in a team situation than in a self-contained situation?

   Easier .... About the same .... More difficult ....

5. Under this program, did you find it easier or more difficult to get help when you needed it?

   Easier .... About the same .... More difficult ....

6. In comparison with the first week, how do you now feel about the possibilities of team teaching?

   Disappointed .... About the same .... Encouraged ....

7. How much value has it been to you professionally to have worked this summer with a team?

   Of little or no value .... Of some value ....

              Of great value ....

8. Check the phrase or phrases which best describe how you feel regarding the role of your team leader and of the principal.

Principal Team Leader

Made too many decisions

Did not make enough
decisions

Easily accessible

Too authoritarian

Too laissez-faire

Did not give enough
direction

Gave good direction and
guidance

Recognized and used
strengths of staff

Comments:

Pupils

1. What seemed to be the attitude of the children during the day?
   More attentive than normal ....
   About the same ....
   Less attentive than normal ....

2. Have you seen some evidence to indicate that some children have
   been disturbed by changing teachers and groups?
   Yes .... No ....

3. Out of the four hours, how much time each day do you feel a teacher
   should have with children from her homeroom?
   Less than 10 minutes ....
   10-20 minutes ....
   20-30 minutes ....
   30-60 minutes ....
   At least an hour ....

4. Of the children from other classes whom you have instructed in a
   classroom situation (not multi-use room), what percent do you feel
   you can call by name? ....

5. Did you find it easier or harder to reach an underachieving or disturbed child?

   Easier .... No difference .... Harder ....

6. From the standpoint of the *pupils,* what do you feel is the greatest value or advantage of team teaching?

Part II

Teachers

1. Would you be willing to work in a team teaching situation during the regular year?

   Yes .... No ....

2. Would you be willing to work in a team teaching situation during a portion of the regular year, rather than the entire year?

   Yes .... No ....

3. Do you feel relaxed and comfortable when planning with others or do you feel it is still somewhat of an emotional strain?

   Relaxed .... Emotional strain ....

4. Were your weak areas balanced by the strengths of other team members?

   Always .... Sometimes .... Usually .... Seldom ....
   Never ....

5. Do you feel you might have done a better or poorer job with another team?

   Better job .... No difference .... Poorer job ....

6. Did interpersonal relations among team members aid cooperative planning?

   Always .... Usually .... Sometimes .... Seldom ....
   Never ....

7. Were you able to work out problems, conflicts, and concerns satisfactorily?

   Always .... Usually .... Sometimes .... Seldom ....
   Never ....

8. Did you feel that you were a vital, contributing member of your team?

   Always .... Usually .... Sometimes .... Seldom ....
   Never ....

9. What do you feel would be the ideal number of teachers to have on a team?

2   3   4   5   6   7   8

10. From the standpoint of the *teacher*:

  a. What has been the greatest value or advantage? ....

  b. What has been the greatest disadvantage or drawback? ....

  c. What has been the greatest source of frustration or irritation? ....

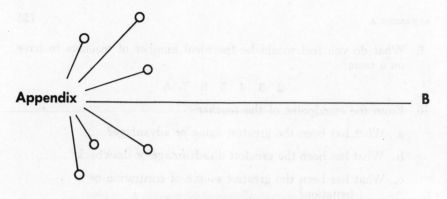

Appendix —————————————————————————————— B

A SIMPLE APPROACH TO ESTABLISH A TEAM
TEACHING PROGRAM

1. Study the available research and literature in this area.
2. Study your own school situation and determine where it needs to be strengthened.
3. Agree on the objectives to be attempted.
4. Study the diverse variations in team teaching and decide which model best suits your own needs.
5. Start team teaching slowly; with one team only with full complement (master teacher, regular teachers, interne-teacher, teacher aide, and clerical aide, plus guidance and counseling assistant).
6. Perhaps it would be best to team in one grade only at first.
7. Combine subject disciplines that have common aspects (American literature — American history or physics-mathematics combinations).
8. Choose team personnel carefully; important factors to be considered are compatability, academic ability (add strength to team in some way) ability to organize ideas, individual flexiblity, enthusiasm for experimentation, and the willingness to work on a team (very important).
9. Prepare team personnel in in-service training for team teaching.
10. Select a team leader who is both a master teacher and leader, and compensate him adequately for the added responsibilities of leadership and duties.
11. Plan, organize and co-ordinate the new curriculum for the team teaching project.
12. Obtain and centralize all new materials needed for the team program (audio-visual aids, books, supplementary materials, etc.).
13. Mark out school facilities for large-group and small-group (seminars) activities that are adequate. This includes a section of the library for independent study.

14. Make a roster of all available community resources that can be used.
15. Prior to beginning team teaching:
   (a) Provide a period of orientation for the parents (includes public relations through press, etc.).
   (b) Provide a period of orientation (several weeks) for the pupils involved in the program.
   (c) Provide a period of orientation (several meetings) for the general staff of the school. Part of this orientation could include the showing of the film (*supra*) "And No Bells Ring."
16. Design new evaluation techniques to suit and meet the objectives of the team teaching program (tests, surveys, periodic evaluations of the program, etc.).
17. With guidance and counseling assistance decide on the standard or basis for grouping students, and incorporate in this standard a method for transferring students in and out of the program.
18. Design a flexible schedule that is really flexible, taking into consideration your present school program, creating large time blocks with the team together in a solid morning or afternoon program. Schedule should include frequent team teacher planning meetings, preparation meetings, counseling of students.[1]

Teachers and Pupils

Teachers on the Team

1. Teacher's strength benefits pupils.

2. Teacher relieved of non-teaching duties can devote more time to his pupils.

The Non-Team Teaching Teacher

1. Teacher is an isolate, and cannot present a complete picture of strength in all areas.

2. Non-team teaching teacher often burdened with many non-teaching duties.

---

[1]Much information for starting a team teaching program can be obtained from "How to Introduce Team Teaching in Your Elementary Schools," *School Management*, V (November, 1961), 58-62 ff; "Team Teaching in the School Program," University of Florida, School of Education (Education Library), Gainesville, Florida, price 20¢; and *Schools for Team Teaching* (ten representative examples), Educational Facilities Laboratories, Inc., 477 Madison Ave., N. Y. 22, N. Y. (no charge); and "The Road to Progress: The Decatur-Lakeview Plan," Decatur, Ill., Public Schools (Sept., 1960). This pamphlet proposes the establishment of a team teaching project.

3. Teacher has time to plan program properly; this benefits the pupils.

3. Time for the non-team teacher is a scarce commodity.

4. The close relationship with the counselor on the team aids the teacher to assist the pupil with his problems.

4. The wide gap between the teacher and the counseling services often is detrimental to the student's welfare.

5. The progress of the pupil is more carefully gauged in a team teaching program, and an effort is made for increased independent study.

5. The pupils often move as a group, and their progress is as a group, not on individual ability.

6. Pupils benefit from the interchange of many ideas because of the teaching team strengths.

6. The intellectual advancement of the pupil is hindered or limited by the abilities of one teacher.

7. Flexible grouping and teacher specialization benefit both the "gifted" pupil and the less able pupil.

7. The fixed traditional program limits the opportunities for the "gifted" and the less able pupil.

8. Stimulation of learning via use of new electronic devices, a diverse curriculum, and new grouping all improve student morale.

8. Conventional programming is limited in its possibility of stimulating learning.

9. Students become responsible, and assume guidance over their program of learning.

9. Often the non-team teacher must urge pupils to be responsible for their learning progress.

10. Small-group instruction (the seminar) offers the pupil the rare opportunity of acquiring knowledge in depth.

10. The non-team teacher finds it difficult to break his class down into small groups.

Model for Elementary School Teaching Team

Two teaching teams may be formed; one for the fourth grade and one for the fifth grade. The personnel could include 120 students, five teachers, four aides, some resource people, interne teacher, and members of the school staff (administrator, counselor, etc.).[2]

The teachers assume responsibility for different parts of the curriculum (language arts, arithmetic, science, music, art, and social studies) according to their specialization and interests.

The pupils are grouped (in flexible patterns) after a careful evaluation process according to their individual needs. The groups may range from 15 to 40 pupils; the number is not fixed.[3]

The teachers are relieved of noninstructional obligations so that they have time for weekly meetings in which the organizational problems of the team are discussed, the curriculum planned, ideas exchanged, and student problems, which arise in the operation of the teaching team, are solved. This is an important phase of team teaching, for it is at this level of team planning that the function of each teacher is clearly defined and the difficulties of the program resolved.

---

[2]For an excellent, tentative cost analysis of team teaching see *Appendix B, The Claremont Teaching Team Program, 1962-63*, Claremont Graduate School & University Center, Claremont, Calif.

[3]See also Donald McNassor, "On Being Learners in Teaching Teams: What Can We Be Sure About?" Claremont Graduate School *Teaching Team Project*, 1962, Claremont, Calif.

TEAM TEACHING BIBLIOGRAPHY

Selected General References

"A Proposal for Flexible Scheduling and Curriculum Organization, Grades 7-12, Language Arts," Dr. William Georgiades, Los Angeles County Office of the Superintendent, 155 W. Washington Blvd., Los Angeles 15.

"Abstracts of Reported Studies of Reorganization of the Professional Staff." In *Studies of Utilization of Staff, Buildings, and Audio-Visual Aids in the Public Schools.* Washington, D. C., National Education Association, 1959, pp. 21-24.

"And No Bells Ring." Film on team teaching produced by the Commission for the Experimental Study of the Utilization of the Staff in the Secondary School. NASSP, 1201 Sixteenth Northwest, Washington 6, D. C. Rental $3.00, 57 minutes, 16mm sound film and TV tape recording.

Catskill Area Project in Small School Design. Oneonta, New York: The Project (215 Home Economics Building, State University College of Education.)

(a) *Catskill Area Project in Small School Design,* 1959. 25 pp. Discussions of multiple classes, flexible schedules, school aides, electronic communications, and shared services.

(b) *School Aides at Work,* 1959. 24 pp. Excellent on the nonprofessional assistant.

(c) *Sharing Educational Services,* 1960. 21 pp.

Central Michigan College of Education and Bay City (Michigan) and Other Public Schools. *A Cooperative Study for the Better Utilization of Teacher Competencies.* 2nd. Printed Report. Mount Pleasant: Central Michigan College of Education, 1955. 32 pp.

Dave Chapman, Inc., Industrial Design. *Design for Educational TV: Planning for Schools with Television.* New York: Educational Facilities Laboratories, 1960. 96 pp.

Claremont Graduate School. *The Claremont Teaching Team Program.* Claremont, Calif., Claremont Graduate School, 1961 and 1962. Project concluded.

"Constructive Use of Teachers' Talents: Symposium," *California Journal of Secondary Education*, XXXV (April, 1960), pp. 232-70. This Symposium includes (12 articles): "Eighth Grade Team Teaching at the Roosevelt Junior High School," by Laurel Jensen et al; "Team Teaching in World Geography, Junior High School," by J. M. Stevens and A. W. Richards; "The Team Teaching Bandwagon," editorial by R. N. Bush.

"A Critical Look at Team Teaching," *Instructor*, LXXI (October, 1961), pp. 39-42.

Decade of Experiment, A ten-year report on the activities of The Fund for the Advancement of Education. The Fund for the Advancement of Education, 477 Madison Avenue, New York 22, N. Y. (no charge).

Education, A Reappraisal, Report on some educational experiments which have received support from The Ford Foundation and its affiliate, The Fund for the Advancement of Education, 477 Madison Avenue, New York 22, N. Y. (no charge).

Educational Facilities Laboratories. *The Cost of A Schoolhouse*. New York: The Laboratories, 477 Madison Avenue, N. Y., 1960. 144 pp. In this volume, pp. 126-39 deal with the questions of school personnel organization.

(a) *Profiles of Significant Schools*: *Schools for Team Teaching* (November, 1960). Describes schools specifically designed for team teaching such as the Grove Street School, Lexington, Mass.

"Experiments in Team Teaching," *Illinois Education*, L (November, 1961), pp. 111-15.

Focus on Change, Guide to Better Schools. Report on the experiments carried out at schools in the United States under the direction of the Commission of the Experimental Study of the Utilization of the Staff in the Secondary School appointed by the National Association of Secondary School Principals. Rand McNally and Co., P. O. Box 7600, Chicago, 80, Ill. (1.25 paper-back).

National Association of Secondary School Principals, National Education Association, Commission on the Experimental Study of the Utilization of the Staff in the Secondary School. Annual Report

1958: *New Horizons in Staff Utilization*, Vol. 42, No. 234.

1959: *Exploring Improved Teaching Patterns*: *Second Report on Staff Utilization*, Vol. 43, No. 24.

1960: *Progressing Toward Better Schools*: *Third Report On Staff Utilization Studies*, Vol. 44, No. 252.

1961: *Seeking Improved Learning Opportunities*: *Fourth Report on Staff Utilization Studies*, Vol. 45, No. 261.

National Education Association. Research Division. "Studies of Utilization of Staff, Buildings, and Audio-Visual Aids in the Public Schools." *Research Report* 1959-R-17, October, 1959. (cost 50¢).

"New Designs for the Secondary School Schedule: Symposium," *California Journal of Secondary Education*, XXXV (February, 1960), pp. 91-134.

New England School Development Council. *Time Allocation in the Elementary School*. Cambridge, Mass.: the Council, April, 1959. 54 pp.

(a) *The Accordion Plan*, February, 1960, 43 pp. The plan involves flexible class size, grouping, co-operative teaching, and differentiated staffing.

Norwalk, Conn., Board of Education, *The Norwalk Plan*: *A Study Designed to Establish New Careers for Teachers*. 93 pp. July, 1959. First report of the team teaching plan in Norwalk.

Oceano School District. *Team Teaching Successful at Oceano*. (A 7-page hectographed report submitted by Supt. A. S. Adams, July 20, 1960 (P. O. Box 407, Oceano, Calif.).

Parent-Teacher Association of Fox Run School, "Team Teaching at Fox Run Elementary School," March, 1961. 50¢ per copy, from Norwalk Plan Coordinating Committee, PTA 228 Fillow Street, Norwalk, Conn.

Phi Delta Kappan. "What Research Says about Teaching and Learning." *Phi Delta Kappan*, XXXIX (March, 1958), pp. 241-304. An excellent article on teaching and learning for both small and large groups, very relevant to team teaching.

"Platoon System of Teaching," *Life Magazine*, LIV, No. 2 (March 22, 1963), pp. 78-89. Discusses the Wayland, Mass. Plan.

Rural Renaissance — Revitalizing Small High Schools, Office of Education Bulletin, 1961, No. 11. Superintendent of Documents, U. S. Gov't Printing Office, Washington 25, D. C. (25¢)

"Symposium: New Opportunities for Expertness; Team Teaching and Flexible Scheduling," *Journal of Secondary Education*, XXXVII (October, 1962), pp. 340-82.

"Team Teaching: A Report of the Pilot Team," Department of Education, Auburn, Maine (September, 1960). Office of the Supervisor of Elementary Education, Chamberlain School, Auburn, Maine, $1.00. On the elementary school team teaching project.

"Team Teaching in the School Program," University of Florida. College of Education (Education Library), Gainesville, Fla. 20¢.

"The Road to Progress: The Decatur-Lakeview Plan," by the Decatur, Ill. Public Schools (September, 1960). This pamphlet proposes the establishment of a team teaching project.

Time, Talent and Teachers. Ford Foundation, 477 Madison Avenue, New York 22, N. Y. (43 pp.), 1960. An excellent description of the innovations assisted by the funds of the Foundation.

Schools for Team Teaching, Ten representative examples. Educational Facilities Laboratories, Inc., 477 Madison Avenue, New York 22, N. Y. (no charge).

"The Shape of Education for 1962-63," *National School Public Relations Association*, NEA, 1962. See especially pp. 25-26, "An Assessment of Team Teaching."

U. S. Office of Education (Washington 25, D. C.) publications related to school organizations:

(a) *The Primary Unit* (December, 1950), 6 p. (#1)
     School Buildings and Equipment for Young Children. (#27)
     Grouping Children for Growth and Learning, (#28).

(b) *Education Brief*.
     No. 5. *Some Types of Classroom Organization*. November, 1955, 6 p.
     No. 35. *Class Enrollment and School Size*, June, 1957, 7 p.

(c) Bulletin 1960, No. 11. *Elementary School Administration and Organization*: *A National Survey of Practices and Policies*.

EXPERIMENTAL PROGRAMS

Director, The Norwalk Plan, Norwalk Public Schools, Norwalk, Conn. (*The Norwalk Plan.*).

Superintendent John Prash, Racine, Wisc.

Superintendent of Schools, Weston, Mass.

Edward J. Anderson, Superintendent of Schools, Wayland, Mass.

John B. Smith, Superintendent of Schools, Greenwich, Conn.

Wisconsin Improvement Program, Teacher Education and Local School Systems, School of Education, The University of Wisconsin, 1120 West Johnson Street, Madison, Wis. (*Making Teaching and Learning Better*).

Paul Perry, Asst. Director, SUPRAD (School and University Program for Research & Development), 6 Everett Street, Cambridge, Mass. (excellent *Bibliography on Team Teaching*).

Education Center, San Diego City Schools, Park and El Cajon Boulevards, San Diego 3, Calif.

Charles Hayes, Director, Team Teaching Project, c/o Leo Weil School, Center Avenue and Soho Street, Pittsburgh 19, Penna. (excellent report: *Pupils, Patterns and Possibilities, 1961 Annual Report.*)

Glenn A. Varner, Asst. Superintendent, Saint Paul Public Schools, Saint Paul, Minn. (*Report on Team Teaching in the Social Studies – John A. Johnson High School*).

Team Teaching Program. Claremont Graduate School, Claremont, Calif. (excellent reports: *The Claremont Team Teaching Program*). Project concluded.

Eugene R. Howard, Superintendent, Ridgewood High School, 7500 West Montrose Avenue, Norridge 34, Ill. (excellent report: *Team Teaching and Staff Utilization in Ridgewood High School – reprint from a National Association of Secondary School Principals Bulletin*).

Superintendent Charles Brown, Newton Public Schools, Newtonville, Mass. (*The Public Schools of Newton, Mass., Annual Report,* 1960-61.)

New England School Development Council, 475 Broadway, Cambridge 3, Mass. (*The Accordion Plan and The Accordion Plan Progress Report,* price 50¢.)

Millard Z. Pond, Superintendent of Schools, Portland, Ore.

Brevard County Project, Dr. B. Frank Brown, Principal, Melbourne High School, 1050 Babcock Street, Melbourne, Fla. (*New Horizons in Learning.*)

Thelma A. McIntosh, Coordinator, Project C: Team Teaching, The College of Education, University of Hawaii, Honolulu, Hawaii. (*Team Teaching in Hawaii's Schools.*)

Architecture and Team Teaching

Anderson, Edward, and Harkness, J. C., "Planned Variability," *The Nation's Schools,* LXV (April, 1960), pp. 83-91. Report of the new high school in Wayland, Mass., designed to accomodate team teaching.

Anderson, Robert H., and Mitchell, Donald P., "Team Teaching, New Learning Concepts Demand Changes in School Plant Design," *The Nation's Schools,* LXV (Spring, 1960), pp. 75-82. Discusses architectural implications of team teaching and takes illustrations from several newly-planned schools designed for team teaching or similar projects. Discusses flexibility and costs.

Educational Facilities Laboratories, Inc., 477 Madison Ave., New York 22, N. Y. *Profiles of Significant Schools.* A series of reports on schools throughout the country whose architectural and educational features make them outstanding.

(a) "Wayland Senior High School, Wayland, Mass.'" (written by Evan Clinchy, Editorial Assistant, January, 1960). Includes a brief description of the team teaching program in Wayland, and how it led to the construction of a high school which was carefully designed for the flexibility essential to a team approach. Included are drawings and floor plans.

(b) "Schools for Team Teaching," 1961, describes several recent and planned elementary and junior high schools designed to house team teaching programs.

"Flexible Classrooms for a Flexible Curriculum," *School Management*, III (November, 1959), pp. 45-47. Comments on the architecture of the Carson City (Michigan) Community School, where there is a team approach to learning.

New Schools for New Education, Educational Facilities Laboratories (New York, 1961). Discusses the architectural implications of J. Lloyd Trump's *Images of the Future*. Based on a workshop conducted by the University of Michigan in 1959 and contains different (ten) approaches to the Trump Plan.

The Pittsburgh Plan, The Pittsburgh School District, Pittsburgh, Penna. This booklet is most valuable to school districts which have old plants and wish to consider renovations. It is an excellent aid to all schools contemplating team teaching.

Price, John W. "More Experience with Utilizing a New School Plant at Syosset, N. Y., Contributing to Staff Use and Curriculum Development." *Bulletin of the National Association of Secondary-School Principals*, XLIII (January, 1959), pp. 167-80. Team teaching in a new school designed for flexibility; many types of arrangements can be used.

Teaching Assistants

Bates, Lorna D. "Need Extra Hours?" *Minnesota Journal of Education*, XXXIX (May, 1959), p. 18.

Bookout, Hamilton H. "Teacher Aids for Lunch-Hour Activities," *School Executive*, LXVIII (February, 1959), p. 136. See also *Education Digest*, XXIV (May, 1959), pp. 26-28.

Braun, R. H., and Steffensen, J. "Grouping, Acceleration, and Teacher Aides, Experiments in Urban Secondary Schools," *National Association of Secondary School Principals Bulletin*, XXXX (January, 1960), pp. 305-315.

Christine, Mrs. Mark, "Parents Lighten the Load at Ohlones School," *National Parent Teacher*, LI (May, 1957), pp. 32-34.

"Community Studies Teacher Aids," *Overview*, I (June, 1960), pp. 77-78.

Cronin, Joseph M., "What's All This About Teacher Aides?" *California Journal of Secondary Education*, XXXIV (November, 1959), pp. 390-397.

Deason, John P., "What They Say about Teacher-Aides," *School Executives*, LXXVII (December, 1957), pp. 59-60.

Duval, Rolland G., "College Seniors Assist Teachers," *Clearing House*, XXXV (November, 1960), p. 162.

Eye, Rev. S. J., "Dixon Plan: Full-Time Paid Aides," *Catholic School Journal, LIX* (November, 1959), pp. 72-73.

French, John H., "Various Methods of Improving Staff Utilization in a Small High School," *National Association of Secondary-School Principals Bulletin,* XXXXI (April, 1957), pp. 261-262.

Gleason, Eleanor M., "Lateral Extension for the Gifted Minds," *National Association of Secondary School Principals Bulletin,* XLII (November, 1958), pp. 94-97.

Gray, Harold F., and Fynboe, C. T., "Teaching Assistants," *California Journal of Secondary Education,* XXXV (April, 1960), pp. 246-249.

Johnson, Curtis, and Vanderhorck, K., "Non-Certified Laboratory Assistants Are Used to Extend Science Opportunities for Pupils at the Alexander Ramsey High School, Roseville, Minn., Second Year," *National Association of Secondary School Principals Bulletin,* XLIII (January, 1959), pp. 12-48.

Lilly, Dorothy B., "What to Do During a Coffee Break," *School and Community,* XLVII (January, 1961), p. 12.

McDaniel, P. William, "Released Time, at No Extra Cost," *Ohio Schools,* XXVII (February, 1959), p. 31.

McGlothlin, Don C., "Three Remedies for the Teacher Shortage," *American School Board Journal,* CXXXV (December, 1957), pp. 21-23.

Mary Alice, Sister, "Teacher-Aides: A Resource; Summary," *National Catholic Education Association Bulletin,* LVI (August, 1959), pp. 309-311.

Mary Carola, Sister, "Working with Teachers' Aides," *Catholic School Journal,* LX (September, 1960), pp. 58-59.

Mary Kenneth, Sister, "Teachers' Aides Really Aid," *Catholic School Journal,* LVII (September, 1957), p. 206.

Mary Lugidia, Sister, "Our Teachers' Aide Program," *Catholic School Journal,* LVII (October, 1957), p. 250.

Nesbitt, William O., and Johnson, P. O., "Some Conclusions Drawn from the Snyder, Texas, Project," *National Association of Secondary School Principals Bulletin,* XLIV (January, 1960), pp. 63-75.

Noall, Matthew G., and Wilson, P., "Paraprofessional Helpers in a Language Arts Program at the Logan City High School, Utah," *National Association of Secondary-School Principals Bulletin,* XLIV (January, 1960), pp. 172-177.

Plutte, William, "We Leave Teachers in Classrooms," *American School Board Journal,* CXLII (March, 1961), p. 16.

Turney, David T., "The Instructional Secretary as Used by Classroom Teachers," Doctoral dissertation, Peabody Research and Development Program, George Peabody College for Teachers, 1959.

Sapp, Eugenia, "Staffing the School Clinic," *National Elementary Principal,* XXXVII (September, 1957), pp. 139-143.

Saunders, Jack O. L., and Sechler, H., "Student Teachers on the Classroom Team," *Elementary School Journal,* LXI (October, 1960), pp. 32-34.

Scanlan, W. J., "Increased Services of Master Teachers Assisted by Cadet Teachers and Clerical Help," *National Association of Secondary-School Principals Bulletin,* XLI (April, 1957), pp. 265-267.

Schaick, Sally Van, "Composition-Reading Machine," *English Journal,* XLIX (April, 1960), pp. 237-241.

Schiffer, Arthur R., "Use of Science Teams," *Science Teacher*, XXVIII (February, 1961), p. 31.

Smith, Edward T., "Teacher Aides — Answer to a Mystery," *Catholic Educator*, XXXI (January, 1961), pp. 369-371.

Thomson, Scott D., "The Emerging Role of the Teacher Aide," *The Clearing House*, XXXVII, No. 6 (February, 1963), pp. 326-331.

Turney, David, "Instructional Secretaries Improve Instruction," *American School Board Journal*, CXL (April, 1960), pp. 19-20.

Turney, David, "Study of the Classroom Use of Secretarial Help in the Public Schools of Davidson County, Tennessee," *National Association of Secondary School Principals Bulletin*, XLIV (January, 1960), pp. 335-340.

Witt, Mrs. Rose M., "Mothers Volunteer as Teachers' Aides," *Catholic School Journal*, LIX (September, 1959), pp. 68-69.

Woodbury, Roger M., "We Tap Our Human Resources," *American School Board Journal*, LXXXV (November, 1957), pp. 33-34.

Zook, N. G., "Menu: A Treat for Teachers," *National Parent Teacher*, LIV (June, 1960), pp. 29-31.

Elementary Schools

"How to Introduce Team Teaching in Your Elementary Schools," *School Management*, V (November, 1961), pp. 58-62 ff.

"How Team Teaching Teams Stopped Double Sessions," *School Management*, VI (March, 1962), pp. 89-92 ff.

A. S. Adams, "Operation Co-Teaching Dateline: Oceano, Calif.," *Elementary School Journal*, LXII (January, 1962), pp. 203-212.

R. H. Anderson and E. A. Hagstrom, and W. M. Robinson, "Team Teaching in an Elementary School," *The School Review*, LXVIII (Pring, 1960), pp. 71-86. Excellent on the Franklin School.

J. M. Bahner, "Reading Instruction in Various Patterns of Grouping in Grades, Four Through Six," *Conference on Reading*, Univ. of Chicago (1959), pp. 95-8.

J. M. Bahner, "Grouping Within A School," *Childhood Education*, XXXVI (April, 1960), pp. 354-6.

H. A. Becker et al, "Team Teaching," *The Instructor*, LXXI (June, 1962), pp. 43-5.

J. A. Brownell and H. A. Taylor, "Theoretical Perspectives for Teaching Teams," *Phi Delta Kappan*, XLIII (January, 1962), pp. 150-7. One of the best reviews on teach teaching models, and team teaching in general.

T. W. Cahall, "Team Teaching in the Elementary School," *Grade Teacher*, LXXVIII (November, 1960), p. 62 ff.

A. S. Fisher, "The Use of Team Teaching in the Elementary School," *School Science and Mathematics*, LXII (April, 1962), pp. 281-88.

John I. Goodland, "News and Comment: In Pursuit of Visions," *Elementary School Journal*, LIX (October, 1958), pp. 1-17. Discusses the need for new practices and looks at projects at Englewood, Fla., Michigan (Flint); Fort Wayne, Ind.; and University City, Mo.

John I. Goodlad, "Experiment in Team Teaching," *Elementary School Journal*, LIX (October, 1958), pp. 11-13.

E. A. Hagstrom, "New Opportunity for Outstanding Teachers," *Grade Teacher* LXXVIII (January, 1961), p 13 ff.

E. G. Horn, "Team Approach Adds Flexibility to Our First-Grade Program," *Illinois Education,* L (November, 1961), pp. 114-15.

W. L. Johnston, "Teamwork in Music Education," *Illinois Education* (April, 1962), p. 324 ff.

A. V. Keliher, "Team Teaching," *High Points,* XLIV (May, 1962), pp. 65-68.

A. W. Lalime, "Elementary Schools Designed for Team Teaching," *Audio-Visual Instructor,* VII (October, 1962), pp. 540-41.

P. Lambert, "Team Teaching for the Elementary School," Educational Leadership, XVIII (November, 1960), pp. 85-8. See also *Education Digest,* XXVI (February, 1961), pp. 5-7.

T. E. Lanning and R. V. Weaver, "Multiple Grouping and Teamwork," *Ohio Schools,* XL (November, 1962), pp. 28-9.

Alan Levensohn, "Team Teaching for the Elementary Schools," *School Management,* II (December, 1958), pp. 45-48. An early description (one of the first) of the Franklin School project during its first year of operation.

J. D. McAulay, "Elementary Education — Five Straws in the Wind," *Phi Delta Kappan, XLI* (June, 1960), pp. 394-96. A fine article on science, homogeneous grouping, content material, departmentalization, and "bigness."

K. J. Rehage, "On the Summer School Circuit," *Elementary School Journal,* LXI (October, 1961), pp. 1-8.

L. Rzepka, "Team Teaching in the Elementary School: What Is it?" *Ohio School,* XL (January, 1962), pp. 14-15 ff.

S. W. Viola, "Team Teaching at Tyrell," *Texas Outlook,* XLVI (November, 1962), pp. 30-01.

W. H. Worth, "Critical Issues in Elementary Education; Team Teaching," *Canadian Education and Research Digest,* II (September, 1962), p. 191.

Yale-Fairfield Study of Elementary Teaching, *Report* 1954-55, New Haven, Connecticut, The Author (February, 1956).

Yale-Fairfield Study of Elementary Teaching, *Teacher Preparation for Mothers Who Are College Graduates.* A Report. New Haven, Conn., 1959.

Yale-Fairfield Study of Elementary Teaching, *Volunteer Service in the Schools.* A guide for the Preparation of a Handbook. New Haven, Conn., 1960.

Junior High School

"Administrative Developments Discussion Groups: Team Teaching," *National Association Secondary School Principals Bulletin,* XLVI (October, 1962), pp. 53-54.

J. Brown et al, "Team Teaching and Large Group Instruction in the Industrial Arts," *Industrial Arts and Vocational Education,* LI (April, 1962), pp. 20-23 ff.

D. H. Battrick, "How Do Team Teaching and Other Staff Utilization Practices Fit Into the Instructional Program of a Junior High School," NAASP *Bulletin,* XLVI (October, 1962), pp. 13-15.

P. B. Glancy, "Brookside Junior High School, Sarasota, Fla., Strives for Quality Education," NASSP *Bulletin,* XLVI (January, 1962), pp. 157-60.

A. L. Hyer, L. D. DuBois, and A. Kain, "We Find Walls Get in the Way; Interview," *Audio-Visual Instructor*, VII (October, 1962), pp. 528-33.

L. Jensen et al, "Eighth Grade Team Teaching at the Roosevelt Junior High School," *California Journal of Secondary Education*, XXXV (April, 1960), pp. 236-43.

J. O. Lorentan, "Team Teaching: Plus and Minus in New York City's Junior High Schools," NASSP *Bulletin*, XLVI (January, 1962), pp. 135-40.

M. F. Noall and G. Rose, "Team Teaching at the Wahlquist Junior High School, Weber County, Utah, NASSP *Bulletin*, XLIV (January, 1960), pp. 164-171.

M. F. Noall and L. Jensen, "Team Teaching at Roosevelt Junior High School, Duchesne County, Utah," NASSP *Bulletin*, XLIV (January, 1960), pp. 156-63.

C. Paullin, "Team Teaching in General Music Classes in San Diego, Calif.," NASSP *Bulletin*, XLVI (January, 1962), pp. 203-07.

G. A. Stetson and J. P. Harrison, "Junior High School Designed for Team Teaching," *American School Board Journal*, CXL (May, 1960), pp. 38-42.

J. M. Stevens and A. W. Richards, "Team Teaching in World Geography, Junior High School," *California Journal Secondary Education*, XXXV (April, 1960), pp. 244-45.

J. C. Stoltenberg, "Team Teaching in Junior High School," *Educational Leadership*, XVIII (December, 1960), pp. 153-55.

R. Swett and P. Dunn Rankin, "Experiment in Team Teaching Seventh Grade Arithmetic," *School Science and Mathematics*, LXII (May, 1962), pp. 341-44.

Team Teaching in the Senior High School[1]

E. J. Anderson and J. C. Harkness, "Planned Variability," *The Nation's Schools*, LXV (April, 1960), pp. 83-91. A report on the new high school in Wayland, Mass., designed to accommodate team teaching.

Henry S. Bissex, "Second Stage: Revision and Extension of Newton Plan Studies," National Association of Secondary School Principals *Bulletin*, XLIII (January, 1959), pp. 104-19.

Henry S. Bissex, "Newton Plan Challenges Traditions of Class Size," *The Nation's Schools*, LXV (March, 1960), pp. 60-4. Discusses the hierarchy of teaching in the Newton Plan in an effort to make use of teaching talents in high school.

W. J. Harrison, "Team Teaching at Muskegon, Mich., Senior High School," National Association of Secondary School Principals *Bulletin*, XLVI (January, 1962), pp. 238-42.

L. Hathaway, "Team Teaching in an Illinois High School," *American Teacher Magazine*, XLVI (April, 1962), pp. 11-12.

Arnold Jackson, "Team Teaching — On A California Senior High School in San Francisco," *Times Supplement*, #2455 (June 8, 1962), p. 1189. This piece discusses team teaching in the high school in special reference to a class in typewriting.

---

[1]For further sources on Team Teaching in the Senior High School see section on Experiments in Team Teaching.

A. J. Nagle, "Team Concept in Organizing a Secondary-School," National Association of Secondary School Principals *Bulletin*, XLIII (April, 1959), pp. 86-7.

Team Teaching in College[2]

R. C. Aden, "Team Teaching at North Texas State University, 1960-61," *Peabody Journal of Education*, XXXIX (March, 1962), pp. 283-87. This is a fine description of team teaching on the collegiate level.

R. Hanvey and M. S. Tenanberg, "University of Chicago Laboratory School, Chicago, Evaluates Team Teaching," National Association of Secondary School Principals *Bulletin*, XLV (January, 1961), pp. 189-97.

A Second Annual *Report* to the Ford Foundation on Team Teaching in Maine, University of Maine, Orono, Maine, 1964.

The Nature and Theory of Team Teaching

John A. Brownell, "The Claremont Teaching Team Program," Claremont Graduate School and University Center *Report*, Claremont, Calif., 1961. Describes the Claremont Program of interdiscipline teams composed of members of various departments. An excellent background description of the assumptions of team teaching.

John A. Brownell and Harris A. Taylor, "Theoretical Perspectives for Team Teaching," *Phi Delta Kappan*, XLIII (January, 1962), pp. 150-157. This is an excellent, comprehensive article on the assumptions and realities of team teaching.

Robert N. Bush, "Team Teaching Bandwagon," *California Journal of Secondary Education*, XXXV (April, 1960), pp. 207-08. This article cautions those who would throw out a judicious approach, and fall blindly in love with team teaching without adapting it properly to their needs.

Robert N. Bush, "Searching Appraisal of New Developments," *Journal of Secondary Education*, XXXVII (October, 1962), pp. 321-6. This is a fine piece of writing which is useful to the researcher of new teaching methods and techniques.

Mary Calhoun, "The Teaching Team," *Child Guidance in Christian Living* (Nashville, Tenn.: Abingdon Press, April, 1959). This piece of writing discusses co-operative teaching as carried on in certain church schools.

J. P. Dix, "Team Teaching Requires Team Spirit," *School and Community*, XLIX (November, 1962), p. 27.

Malcolm P. Douglass, "Team Teaching: Fundamental Change or Passing Fancy," California Teachers Association *Journal*, XIX, No. 2 (March, 1963), pp. 26-9, 55-6. This is an excellent article which reviews the stereotypes surrounding team teaching.

Robert S. Gilchrist, "Promising Practices in Education," *Phi Delta Kappan*, XLI (February, 1960), pp. 208-11; and (March, 1960), pp. 269-74.

M. J. Gillers, "One-Way Ticket to the Moon!" *High Points*, XLIII (May, 1961), pp. 67-8.

---

[2]For further sources on Team Teaching in College see section on the Experiments in Team Teaching.

R. O. Hahn, Jack Nelson, and Gertrude Robinson, "Team Teaching: A Second Look," *The Journal of Teacher Education* (NEA), XII (December, 1961), pp. 508-10.

Warren Hamilton and W. Rehwoldt, "By Their Differences They Learn," *National Elementary Principal*, XXXVII (December, 1957), pp. 27-9. This is a public report of the multigrade, multi-age grouping plan in Torrance, Calif.; although the nongraded concept and team teaching are not included in the Torrance Plan, the Plan is a significant departure from conventional school organization.

Anne Hoppach, "Team Teaching: Form Without Substance?" National Education Association *Journal*, L (April, 1961), pp. 47-8. This is a fine article which examines team teaching with a critical eye.

M. D. Lobb, M. F. Moall, and H. L. Slichenmyer, "What Are Some Promising Practices in Team Teaching?" National Association of Secondary School Principals *Bulletin*, XLIV (April, 1960), pp. 2-7. This is an article worth examining for those contemplating team teaching projects.

Helen H. Long, "What Price Parent Participation?" In *Parents and the Schools*. National Education Association, Department of Elementary School Principals, 36th *Yearbook*, Washington, D. C., The Association, 1957.

R. Marsch, "Team Teaching — New Concept?" *Clearing House*, XXXV (April, 1961), pp. 496-99.

W. B. Mitchell, "Why Try Team Teaching?" National Association of Secondary School Principals *Bulletin*, XLVI (January, 1962), pp. 247-52.

W. S. Norton, "Approaches to Team Teaching," National Association of Secondary School Principals *Bulletin*, XLIV (October, 1960), pp. 89-92. This article explains several diverse approaches to team teaching which could prove valuable to those experimenting with team teaching.

Robert D. Ohm, "Toward a Rationale for Team Teaching," *Administrator's Notebook*, IX, No. 7 (March, 1961). This is a critical analytical article on team teaching which makes many important distinctions among types of teams.

C. H. Peterson, "Is Team Teaching for Your Schools?" *American School Board Journal*, CXLV (October, 1962), pp. 11-13. This article reviews the conditions upon which team teaching may depend, and asks the important questions which should be answered before jumping on the team teaching bandwagon.

P. R. Pitruzzello, "What Is Happening in the Use of Teacher Teams and Teacher Assistants: Report of A Survey," National Association of Secondary School Principals *Bulletin*, XLV (April, 1961), pp. 326-8. This article discusses the nature of teacher teams and sheds some light on the various obligations of teacher assistants.

P. R. Pitruzzello, "Report On Team Teaching," *The Clearing House*, XXXVI (February, 1962), pp. 333-6. This article gives a more than adequate summary on the substance of team teaching.

M. E. Ploghoft, "Another Look at Team Teaching," *The Clearing House*, XXXVI (December, 1961), pp. 219-21.

Nicholas C. Polos, "Progress in Teacher Education; the Claremont Plan," *Journal of Teacher Education* (NEA), XI (September, 1960), pp. 398-401. This analytical article describes the Claremont (Calif.) Plan which revolves around the "seed corn" concept of obtaining superior teachers.

Nicholas C. Polos, "The Teaching Team in Action," *California Journal of Secondary Education,* XXXVI, No. 7 (November, 1961) pp. 415-19. This article discusses the use of team teaching to individualize instruction, examines critically some of its concepts, and makes observations on the future of team teaching.

Judson T. Shaplin, "Team Teaching," *Saturday Review,* XLIV (May 20, 1961), pp. 54-5, 70. A discussion of the pitfalls in team teaching and the elements common to many team teaching projects.

Robert L. Shayon, radio program on team teaching in the EVERYBODY'S MOUNTAIN Series of the National Association of Educational Broadcasters, 14 Gregory Hall, Urbana, Ill. Tape available on a rental basis.

Mark R. Shedd, "Team Teaching: Why and Now," *Maine Teacher,* XX (May, 1960), pp. 16-7. This is a report on the Auburn Project.

Mark R. Shedd, "Team Teaching and Its Impact Upon the Role of the Elementary School Principal," *Maine Elementary School Principals Newsletter,* April, 1960.

Harris A. Taylor, "Claremont Graduate School Program for Team Teaching," *High School Journal,* XLIII (February, 1960), 277-82. This is a first-rate article on the Claremont Program for Team Teaching which offers valuable advice on team teaching. Project concluded.

G. W. Wagner, "Team Teaching," *Education,* LXXXI (May, 1961), pp. 572-3.

On the Merits of Team Teaching — Pro and Con

R. H. Anderson, "Three Samples of Team Teaching in Action," *The Nation's Schools,* LXV (May, 1960), pp. 102-110. This is a useful article which explains team teaching with the proper emphasis.

R. H. Anderson, "Team Teaching," National Education Association *Journal,* I, No. 3 (March, 1961), pp. 52-54. This is a fine article which describes some sample projects and discusses some of the merits of team teaching.

I. Bodine et al, "Contribution to Team Teaching," National Association of Secondary Schools Principals *Bulletin,* XLVI (April, 1962), pp. 111-17. This article offers some useful information on the advantages of team teaching.

J. J. B. Dempster, "America Explores Team Teaching," *Times Educational Supplement,* 2449 (April 27, 1962), p. 826. Mr. Dempster is the Chief Educational Officer, Southampton, England. The team teaching project in America is given a British examination; the observations are extremely valuable.

W. Dagnell, "Team Teaching," *The Times Educational Supplement,* 2453 (May 25, 1962), p. 1080.

S. E. Dean, "Team Teaching: A Review," *School Life,* XLIV (September, 1961), pp. 5-8. This article contains some useful information on team teaching and is also to be found in *Education Digest,* XXVII (December, 1961), pp. 21-3.

H. D. Drummond, "Team Teaching: An Assessment," *Educational Leadership,* XIX (December, 1961), pp. 160-6. This is a good review of team teaching and can be found in the *Education Digest,* XXVII (February, 1962), pp. 5-8.

Stanley Edwards, "Team Teaching," *The Times Educational Supplement*, 2450 (May 4, 1962), p. 883. Team teaching seen through British eyes.

S. R. Jonsson, "Team Teaching? Enthusiasm Is High," New York State Education *Bulletin*, L (November, 1962), pp. 14-6.

Stanley J. Keach, "Team Teaching Is Exciting!" *International Journal of Religious Education*, XXXIV (September, 1957), pp. 12-3.

G. W. Maxwell et al, "How Effective Is Team Teaching in General Business?" *Business Education World*, XLII (December, 1961), pp. 7-10.

D. McCuskey, "Critical Commentary," Association for Student Teaching *Yearbook*, 1961, pp. 92-4.

J. W. R. Stone, "Team Teaching," *The Times Educational Supplement*, #2451 (May 11, 1962), p. 953.

J. W. R. Stone, "Team Teaching," *The Times Educational Supplement*, #2454 (June 1, 1962), p. 1139. These two articles give some insight on team teaching as seen by a British observer.

William J. Stone and William K. Ramstad, "Team Teaching — The Results of a California Survey," *California Journal of Secondary Education*, XXXVI, No. 5 (May, 1961), pp. 273-2.

W. Walker, "Team Teaching: Pros and Cons," California Teachers Association *Journal*, LVIII (April, 1962), p. 17. This is a useful assessment of team teaching.

Thomas M. Weiss and M. S. Morris, "Critique of the Team Approach," *Educational Forum*, XXIV (January, 1960), pp. 207-08.

Paul Woodring et al, "Education in America," a S. R. Supplement, *Saturday Review*, XLIII (Sept. 17, 1960), pp. 65-94. This is a collection of articles by Woodring, A. D. Morse, Harold Howe, and others, and represents an argument for team teaching. This is the first in a series of monthly education departments in this magazine, and much current information can be found in the *Saturday Review* series.

Teachers Look at Team Teaching

G. C. Ackerlund, "Some Teacher Views on the Self-Contained Classroom," *Phi Delta Kappan*, XL (April, 1959), pp. 283-5. This piece discusses the traditional classroom organization and possible future arrangements.

J. S. Butterweck, "Teachers on A Team," *Pennsylvania School Journal*, LVI (October, 1957), p. 57.

Ned Hoopes, "Team Teachers Play A Winning Game," Parent Teacher Association *Magazine*, LV (May, 1961), pp. 29-31.

J. J. Howell, et al, *Teaching Fellows*. Yale-Fairfield Study of Elementary Teaching, New Haven, Connecticut, 1960.

In-Service Training and Team Teaching

Richard W. Elliott, "Team Teaching Effective In-Service Training," *American School Board Journal*, LXLIV, No. 2 (February, 1962), p. 19.

J. Nelson et al, "Team Teaching for Teacher Education: the New Approach," *Journal of Teacher Education*, XII (September, 1961), pp. 380-82

Bryce Perkins and G. A. Prescott, "New Careers for Teachers," *Connecticut Teacher*, XXVI (April, 1959), pp. 4-5. This piece describes the roles of team leader and co-operating teacher as they are being developed in the Norwalk Plan team teaching project.

M. R. Sabath and E. H. Moore, "Team Teaching in Teacher Education," Association for Student Teaching *Yearbook*, 1961, pp. 86-91.

T. C. Tollefson, "We Use Team Teaching Assignments to Help Beginning Teachers," *Illinois Education*, L (November, 1961), p. 115.

Paul Woodring, *New Directions in Teacher Education.* New York: Fund for the Advancement of Education, 1957, 142 pp. This book deals primarily with teacher education, but the last chapter does discuss how team teaching may fit into a program developing professional skills.

Staff Utilization and Team Teaching

D. Baynham, "Selected Staff Utilization Projects in California, Georgia, Colorado, Illinois, Michigan and New York," National Association Secondary School Principals *Bulletin*, XLVI (January, 1962), pp. 14-98. A fine review of team teaching projects in various parts of the United States and their results.

Lee L. Bloomenshine, "San Diego Uses the Teaching Team Approach in Staff Utilization," National Association of Secondary School Principals *Bulletin*, XLIII (January, 1959), pp. 217-19. This article describes team teaching in four schools.

Lee L. Bloomenshine and T. M. Brown, "San Diego, Calif., Conducts Two-Year Experiments with Team Teaching," National Association of Secondary School Principals *Bulletin*, XLV (January, 1961), pp. 146-66.

Lee L. Bloomenshine, "Team Teaching in San Diego — The First Year," National Association of Secondary School Principals *Bulletin*, XLIV (January, 1960), pp. 181-96.

C. L. Dillon, "Taylorville, Ill., Senior High School Uses Tape Recorders, Team Teaching, and Large Group Instructions to Improve Staff Utilization," National Association of Secondary School Principals *Bulletin*, XLV (January, 1961), pp. 178-9.

M. P. Heller and E. Belford, "Team Teaching and Staff Utilization in Ridgewood High School," National Association of Secondary School Principals *Bulletin*, XLVI (January, 1962), pp. 105-22. This is a valuable piece of writing about staff utilization at a school which has gone all out for team teaching.

J. Menacker, "Inter-Departmental Team Teaching in the High School," *Education Digest*, XXVI (May, 1961).

A. R. Partridge, "Staff Utilization in Senior High School," *Educational Leadership*, XVIII (January, 1961), pp. 217-21.

John Price, William C. French and E. R. Weinrich, "Some Influences of a New School on Planning Staff Use and Curriculum Development are Studied in Syosset, New York," National Association of Secondary School Principals *Bulletin*, XLII (January, 1958), pp. 154-64.

I. J. Singer, "Survey of Staff Utilization Practices in Six States," NASSP *Bulletin* (January, 1962), pp. 1-13.

D. R. Wynn and R. W. DeRemer, "Staff Utilization, Development, and Evaluation," *Review of Educational Research*, XXXI (October, 1961), pp. 393-400.

Instruction and Team Teaching

R. H. Anderson, "Organizing Groups for Instruction," National Social Study Education *Yearbook*, 1961, part 1, pp. 239-64.

P. H. Falk, "The Improvement of Instruction," *The Bulletin*, XXX, No. 1. Madison Education Association, Madison, Wis., April, 1960. This fine article warns of the dangers of leaping on a team teaching bandwagon before it has been thoroughly tried and tested.

W. J. Gambold, ed., "Modern Teacher and New Media of Instruction," *Education*, LXXXIII (October, 1962), pp. 67-70.

John M. Hahner, "Grouping Within a School," *Childhood Education*, XXXVI (April, 1960), pp. 354-6. This article scrutinized a number of traditional concepts, including the one that a single teacher must always work with approximately 30 pupils.

Harold Howe II, "Curriculum, The Team and the School: An examination of Relationships," *California Journal of Secondary Education*, XXXVII (October, 1962), pp. 353-61.

William M. Mahoney, "To Improve the Teaching-Learning Process — Try Coordinate Teaching," *American School Board Journal*, CXXXIX (November, 1959), pp. 13-14. Discusses the sixth grade in Norton, Mass., and the capitalization on the special interests of teachers.

William K. Ramstad, "An Instructional System," *Journal of Secondary Education*, XXXVIII, No. 1 (January, 1963), pp. 19-20.

W. J. Wrightstone, *Class Organization for Instruction*. What Research Says to the Teacher, No. 13. Prepared by the American Educational Research Association in cooperation with the Department of Classroom Teachers, Washington, D. C.: NEA, May, 1957, 33 pp. This is a brief summary of the research relating to class organization, with implications for the studies of grouping patterns.

Learning and Team Teaching

Edward B. Fry, G. L. Bryan and Joseph W. Rigney, *Teaching Machines*: *An Annotated Bibliography*. Supplement to Audio-Visual Communication Review. Washington, D. C.: NEA, Department of Audio-Visual Instruction, 1960, 80 pp. This piece contains some excellent ideas on electronic learning which can be used with team teaching.

R. Marsch, "New Technique Has Advantages for Both Students and Teachers," *Illinois Education*, L (November, 1961), pp. 111-12.

L. W. Nelson, "New Ideas in Education," *Harvard Graduate School of Education Association*, IV (September, 1959), pp. 11-16. The thesis of this article is that new conditions of life and new technologies require equally new and immediate ideas in education.

R. H. Nelson, "And Here Is How an Educator Would Put the Perception Core into Effective Use," *The Nation's Schools*, LXV (March, 1960), pp. 85-87.

Floyd Rinker, "Subject Matter, Students, Teacher, Methods of Teaching, and Space Redeployed in the Newton, Mass., High School," NASSP *Bulletin*, XLIII (January, 1958), pp. 69-80. Discusses Newton's large-group lecture project (first article).

L. J. Stiles, "Individual and Team Teaching," *Wisconsin Journal of Education,* XCII (January, 1960), pp. 7-10, 13.

George D. Stoddard, "The Dual Progress Plan," *School and Society,* LXXXVI (October 11, 1958), pp. 351-52. This is not a team teaching project but similarities will be noted in philosophy and operations (involves graded nonspecialist classes and nongraded specialist classes).

Flexible Scheduling and Team Teaching

V. Cordry, "More Flexible Schedule at Fremont," *California Journal of Secondary Education,* XXXV (February, 1960), pp. 114-16.

R. H. Johnson et al, "Continued Study of Class Size, Team Teaching and Scheduling in Eight High Schools in Jefferson County, Colo. (School District No. R-1, Lakewood, Colo.)," NASSP *Bulletin,* CCXLIII (January, 1959), pp. 99-103.

R. H. Johnson and M. D. Lobb, "Transformation of the Sacred Secondary School Schedule," *California Journal of Secondary Education,* XXXV (February, 1960), pp. 96-105. This piece discusses flexible scheduling and the "Golden Plan."

R. H. Johnson, M. D. Lobb, and Floyd G. Swenson, "An Extensive Study of Team Teaching and Schedule Modification in Jefferson County, Colo., School District R-1," NASSP *Bulletin,* XL (January, 1960), pp. 79-93. This article contains some very valuable hints on team teaching and flexible scheduling.

W. J. Stone, "New Designs for Secondary-School Scheduling," *California Journal of Secondary Education,* XXXV (February, 1960), pp. 126-30.

Facilities for Team Teaching

Evans, Clinchy, *Profiles of Significant Schools: Wayland Senior High School, Wayland, Mass.* New York: Educational Facilities Laboratories, January, 1960, 28 pp. This is an important piece on facilities and team teaching. It includes drawings and floor plans for flexibility so essential to a team approach, and describes the team teaching program at Wayland and its new high school.

P. Lewis, "Facilities for the School of the Future: A Bibliography," *Audio-Visual Instructor,* VII (October, 1962), pp. 562-5. This is a fine, useful piece which is most valuable and would be helpful to anyone planning team teaching.

Alice Miel, "The Self-Contained Classroom: An Assessment," *Teachers College Record,* LIX (February, 1958), pp. 282-91. Advocates a modified self-contained classroom with the teacher as home-base leader aided by machines, materials, and school aides.

Gertrude Smith, "Experimentation at Verdugo Hills High School," *California Journal of Secondary Education,* XXXVI (November, 1961), pp. 433-40.

Administering Team Teaching

A. B. Clark, "Administering Team Teaching in the East Side District, San Jose, Calf.," NASSP *Bulletin,* XLVI (January, 1962), pp. 141-44.

Luvern L. Cunningham, "Keys to Team Teaching," *Overview*, II, No. 2 (October, 1960), pp. 54-55. This article points out the administrative problems which may be encountered in the kind of staff deployment involved in team teaching.

Luvern L. Cunningham, "Team Teaching: Where Do We Stand?" *Administrator's Notebook*, Midwest Administration Center, University of Chicago, VIII, (April, 1960), 8 pp. This is a clear, and concise explanation of the various categories of team teaching.

T. C. Gurney, M. Bleifeld, J. E. Reese, and A. K. Link, "What Responsibilities for the Principal in Organizing, Supervising, and Evaluating Teaching Teams?" NASSP *Bulletin*, XLV (April, 1961), pp. 115-20.

Harold Howe II, "The High School Principal in Newton, Mass., Reacts to Redeployment," NASSP *Bulletin*, XLIV (January, 1960), pp. 122-38. This article discusses the role of the administrator in a large group project.

Mark R. Shedd, "Team Teaching and Its Impact Upon the Role of the Elementary School Principal," *Maine Elementary School Principals Newsletter*, April, 1960.

Experiments in Team Teaching in Various Subject Areas

John M. Bahner, "In Grades Four Through Six," *Reading Instruction in Various Patterns of Grouping*. Proceedings of the Annual Conference on Reading, University of Chicago, 1959, pp. 95-8. Discusses reading techniques in the Englewood team teaching plan (Sarasota, Fla.).

John M. Bahner, "Grouping Within A School," *Childhood Education*, XXXVI (April, 1960), pp. 354-56. A second article on the Englewood project in Sarasota, Fla. Program (Sarasota County).

L. C. Bergner, "Team Teaching in Typewriting," *American Business Education*, XVIII (May, 1962), pp. 249-51.

V. Bernucci and M. Hartdegen, "How to Use Team Teaching in Industrial Arts," *Industrial Arts and Vocational Education*, L (January, 1961), pp. 18-20.

W. G. Bovinet, "Intern Program, Team Teaching and Language Laboratory at Glenbrook High School," NASSP *Bulletin*, XLIII (January, 1959), pp. 249-54.

G. G. Bruntz, "Team Approach to Social Science Teaching," *High School Journal*, XLIII (April, 1960), pp. 370-74.

W. G. Carpenter, "Team Teaching in Basic Business," *Balance Sheet*, XLII (February, 1961), pp. 279 ff.

H. A. Clawson, "Science Lecture and Team Approaches in English at Mattoon Senior High School," NASSP *Bulletin*, XLIII (January, 1959), pp. 245-57.

H. A. Clawson, "English and Science Studies in the Mattoon Senior High School," NASSP *Bulletin*, XLIV (January, 1960), pp. 257-63.

H. A. Clawson, "Mattoon, Ill. High School, Tries Team Teaching and Science Orientation," NASSP *Bulletin*, XLV (January, 1961), pp. 92-99.

E. M. Cobett, "Different Approach to Team Teaching," *Ohio Schools*, XXXVIII (November, 1960), pp. 10-11.

Charles R. Colbert, "Perception Core School," *The Nation's Schools*, LXV (March, 1960), pp. 79-84.

W. L. Cooper, "The Use of Tapes, Language Laboratory, and Teaching Teams at the J. Sterling Morton High School and Junior College," NASSP *Bulletin*, XLIV (January, 1960), pp. 233-43.

W. L. Cooper, "J. Sterling Morton High School and Junior College, Cicero, Ill., Uses Tapes, Language Laboratories, and Team Teaching," NASSP *Bulletin*, XLV (January, 1961), pp. 79-84.

C. W. Cope and W. Medley, "Winfield, Kansas, High School Pioneers Team Teaching," NASSP *Bulletin*, XLVI (January, 1962), pp. 166-72. This article offers many useful suggestions on team teaching.

E. Crandell and W. Piel, "Birmingham Tries Team Teaching Experiment,' *Michigan Education Journal*, XXXVIII (January, 1961), pp. 344-5 ff.

H. D. Drummond, "Experiment at Norwalk," *Newsweek*, LIII (June 8, 1959), p. 54.

G. A. Eakin, and E. S. Spence, "Team Teaching and Independent Reading," *Elementary English*, XXXIX (March, 1962), pp. 266-8.

R. D. Elliott and E. P. Gamble, "Evanston, Ill., Township High School Adds to Its Program; Health Education with Team Teaching," NASSP *Bulletin*, LVI (January, 1962), pp. 266-8.

P. M. Ford, "Different Day for the English Teacher," *English Journal*, L (May, 1961), pp. 334-37.

John R. Ginther and William A. Shroyer, "Team Teaching in English and History at the 11th Grade Level," *The School Review*, LXX, No. 3 (Autumn, 1962), pp. 303-314.

C. E. Gross, "Team Teaching in Pittsburgh," *Education Digest*, XXVIII (November, 1962), pp. 12-15.

Richard E. Gross, "Emerging Horizons for the Social Studies," *Social Education*, XXIV (January, 1960), pp. 21-4. This is an excellent article on the future of the Social Studies. (Lewis Paul Todd, 1201 16th St., No. West, Washington 6, D. C.)

M. Hanhila, "Double-Sized Class Opinionaire: A Report On A Team Teaching Experiment," *Arizona Teacher*, LI (September, 1962), pp. 12-13.

C. Hayes, "Community Services Backstop Pittsburgh Teaching Teams," *Audio-visual Instructor*, VII (June, 1962), pp. 390-1.

Will Hemeyer and Jean B. McGrew, "Big Ideas for Big Classes," *The School Review*, LXCIII (Autumn, 1960), pp. 308-17. This piece describes associate teaching used in the Rich Township High School, Park Forest, Ill. The article distinguishes between co-ordinate teaching and associate teaching and contains some useful suggestions on teaching methods.

C. T. Hoan and R. C. Adams, "Experimentation at Fremont High School," *California Journal of Secondary Education*, XXXVII (May, 1962), pp. 274-9.

J. Hoffman, "Team Teaching Spells Progress in Business Education," *Business Education World*, XLII (September, 1961), pp. 12-13 ff.

J. H. Hull, "Multigrade Teaching," *The Nation's Schools*, LXII (July, 1958), pp. 33-36. This is a description of the Torrance, Calif., multi-grade plan.

W. Hurley et al, "Team Teaching and the Use of Recorders in Taylorville Senior High School," NASSP *Bulletin*, XLIV (January, 1960), pp. 268-74.

R. H. Johnson and R. Shutes, "Biology and Team Teaching," *American Biology Teacher*, XXIV (April, 1962), pp. 247-55.

D. Kaltenbach, "Experiment in Team Teaching," *Ohio Schools*, XXXIX (October, 1961), pp. 15 ff.

F. C. Mayer and J. H. Wooldridge, "Preparing for Team Teaching at West Clermont," *American School Board Journal*, CXLV (July, 1962), p. 10.

T. E. McCollum et al, "Snyder, Texas, Continues Team Teaching," NASSP *Bulletin*, XLV (January, 1961), pp. 261-65.

Arthur D. Morse, "Team Teaching in Action: The Franklin School in Lexington, Mass." In *Schools of Tomorrow — Today*. New York: Doubleday Co., 1960, pp. 9-26.

Arthur D. Morse (producer), "The Influential American" television program in *CBS Reports* series, presented November 13, 1960. A part of this program shows team teaching at the Franklin School, Lexington, Mass. Transcripts are available from CBS News, 485 Madison Ave., New York 22, N. Y.

Arthur D. Morse, *School of Tomorrow — Today*. New York: Doubleday and Co., 575 Madison Avenue, Sept., 1960. This is a valuable book of 191 pages which offers a great deal of information on team teaching and the many projects (Franklin School, Appleton, Wisc., Bay City, Mich., Catskill Project, and the Harvard Teacher-Preparation Programs).

W. O. Nesbitt and P. O. Johnson, "Some Conclusions Drawn from the Snyder, Texas Project," NASSP *Bulletin*, XLIV (January, 1960), pp. 63-75.

W. O. Nesbitt, "Big Classes in Texas," *Educational Screen*, XXXVIII (November, 1959), pp. 594-96.

M. F. Noall and Rose Gale, "Team Teaching at the Wahlquist Junior High School, Weber County, Utah," NASSP *Bulletin*, XLIV (January, 1960), pp. 164-71.

M. C. O'Brien, "California Surveys Experimental Programs in Business Education," NASSP *Bulletin*, XLVI (January, 1962), pp. 99-102. This fine article describes team teaching in an important area of modern education.

Barbara S. Pannwitt, "Evanston, Ill., Township High School Reports on Five Years of Projects, Including Television, Team Teaching, and Large and Small Group Instruction," NASSP *Bulletin*, XLV (January, 1961), pp. 244-48.

G. E. Patterson, L. G. Swenson, and Robert H. Johnson, "Classes of 10, 20, 35, and 70 Under Varied Conditions Are Taught in Jefferson County, Colo., To Discover Effects on Students and Teachers," NASSP *Bulletin*, XLII (January, 1958), pp. 165-67. Presents the hypotheses that were tested in the Jefferson County project, and the results shed some light on grouping problems.

C. Paullin, "Team Teaching in General Music Classes in San Diego," *California Journal of Secondary Education*, XXXVI (March, 1961), pp. 133-7. This article discusses an area of team teaching which has not been given much attention.

Bryce Perkins et al, "Teamwork Produces Audio-Visual Techniques," *Grade Teacher*, LXXVII (June, 1960), pp. 55-72.

Bryce Perkins, "Team Teaching," *Educational Perspectives* (February, 1962), p. 2.

J. R. Powers and S. Oudot, "Parlons Français," *Educational Leadership*,

XVII (December, 1959), pp. 148-52. This article describes the uses of television and language.

J. Schneider, G. Deinlein, J. Cosgrove, and M. J. Ramos, "Team Teaching at Chaminade High School, Dayton, Ohio," National Catholic Education Association *Bulletin*, LIX (August, 1962), pp. 314-17.

H. G. Shane, "Grouping in the Elementary School," *Phi Delta Kappan*, XLI (April, 1960), pp. 313-19. This is a summary of the many kinds of grouping which educators find useful.

R. M. Sichels et al, "Speech Teachers Team Up to Improve The Sophomore Course," *Illinois Education*, L (November, 1961), pp. 113-14.

A Sivon et al, "Experiment in Team Teaching," *Ohio Schools*, XXXIX (March, 1961), pp. 34-5.

Gertrude Smith et al, "Team Teaching, A Challenge to Change," *Arizona Teacher*, L (November, 1961), pp. 20-4.

V. Smith, "Team Teaching in Geometry," NASSP *Bulletin*, XLVI (March, 1962), pp. 97-99. See also *School and Community*, XLVIII (April, 1962), p. 13 ff. This is a very interesting article on a team teaching project on a subject about which very little has been written.

V. H. Smith, "Team Teaching Has Advantages," *The English Journal* (April, 1960), pp. 242-4. This article describes team teaching in Lakewood, Colo., and its advantages for teaching of English.

E. D. Stevens, "Coatsville's Project Pyramid," *Pennsylvania School Journal*, LVIII (November, 1959), pp. 94-5.

John M. Stevens and A. W. Richards, "Team Teaching in World Geography, Junior High School," *California Journal of Secondary Education*, XXXV (April, 1960), pp. 244-45.

P. Tedesco, "Team Teaching in Typing," *Journal of Business Education*, XXXVIII (October, 1960), pp. 10-11. Here is an example of team teaching which is valuable and on a subject about which little has been written.

P. Tedesco, "Team Teaching: Some Experimental Results," *American Business Education*, XVIII (May, 1962), pp. 245-8. This article is of great value to those interested in business education.

E. Tracy and C. H. Peterson, "Easton, Penn., Team Teaching Programs," NASSP *Bulletin*, XLVI (January, 1962), pp. 145-56. Anyone interested in team teaching projects will find Volume 46 of the National Association of Secondary School Principals *Bulletin* very useful in describing various projects.

G. F. Varner, "Team Teaching in Johnson High School, St. Paul, Minn.," NASSP *Bulletin*, XLVI (January, 1962), pp. 161-6.

Harvey R. Wall and Robert W. Reasoner, *Team Teaching* (Concord, Calif., 1962). This booklet can be obtained from the Mt. Diablo School District, and is a valuable description of team teaching on various levels and the results of one project.

J. O. Ward, "Another Plan for Co-ordinate Teaching," *American School Board Journal*, CXL (February, 1960), p. 10.

Lerue Winget et al, "What Are Some Experimental Changes in. . .?" NASSP *Bulletin*, XLIII (April, 1959), pp. 108-12.

J. H. Woolbridge and F. E. Mayer, "Building for Team Teaching," *Ohio Schools*, XL (May, 1962), p. 15.

The Future of Team Teaching

D. Baynham, "School of the Future in Operation," *Phi Delta Kappan,* XLII (May, 1961), pp. 350-54.

B. G. Connor, "Let Your Enthusiasm Show," *The English Journal,* L (December, 1961), pp. 626-8.

H. D. W. Conner, "Team Teaching Program," *The Virginia Journal of Education,* LIV (March, 1961), p. 13.

Francis S. Chase, "The Schools I Hope to See," National Education Association *Journal, XLVI* (March, 1957), pp. 164-66.

Arthur R. King Jr., "Planning for Team Teaching: The Human Considerations," *California Journal of Secondary Education,* XXXVII (October, 1962), pp. 362-67. This is a first-rate article on an important phase of team teaching. It contains some excellent suggestions written by a man who has had a wealth of experience in team teaching.

R. A. Larmee and R. Ohn, "University of Chicago Laboratory School Freshman Project Involves Team Teaching, New Faculty Position and Regrouping of Students," NASSP *Bulletin,* XLIV (January, 1960), pp. 275-89.

C. H. Peterson, "Eastern Senior High School Team Teaching Program," Easton-Forks Joint School System and Easton Area Joint High School System, Easton, Pennsylvania, *Curriculum Publications SE-60-1 (1960).* This is a concentrated description of a team teaching program for students of high ability, and contains some excellent suggestions for future practices.

Lloyd J. Trump, three pamphlets for the Commission on the Experimental Study of the Utilization of the Staff in the Secondary School:

(a) *An Exciting Profession: New Horizons for Secondary School Teachers* (1957). Discusses the various aspects of staff utilization, and lists possible experimental studies, 34 pp.

(b) *Images of the Future* (1959). Describes what the secondary school of tomorrow might be like by combining many of the significant trends observable today.

(c) *New Directions to Quality Education: The Secondary School of Tomorrow* (1960). An outline of the major directions improvements have been taking in the secondary schools today.

INDEX